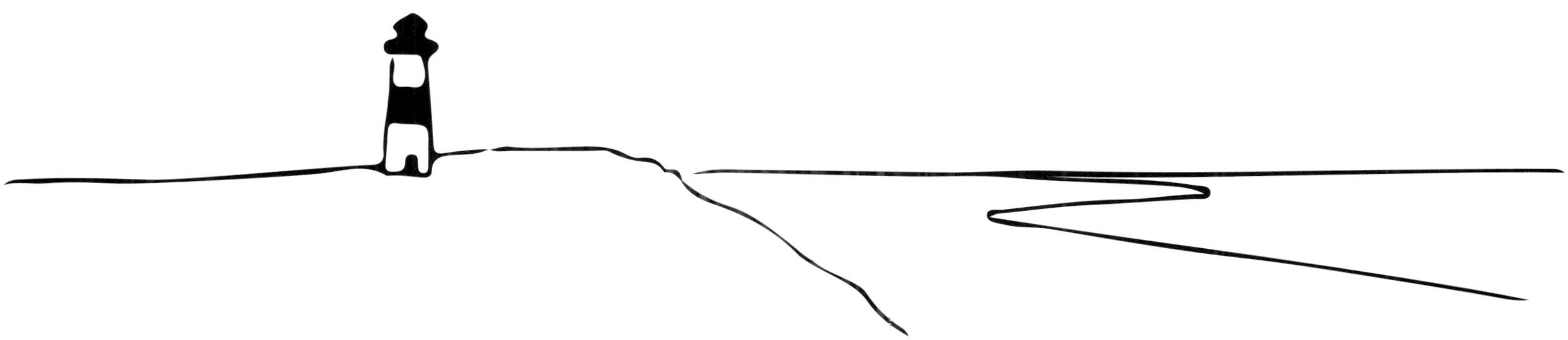

FRANK WAGNER MARKUS TOLLHOPF SABINE VATTERODT

SEHN SUCHT

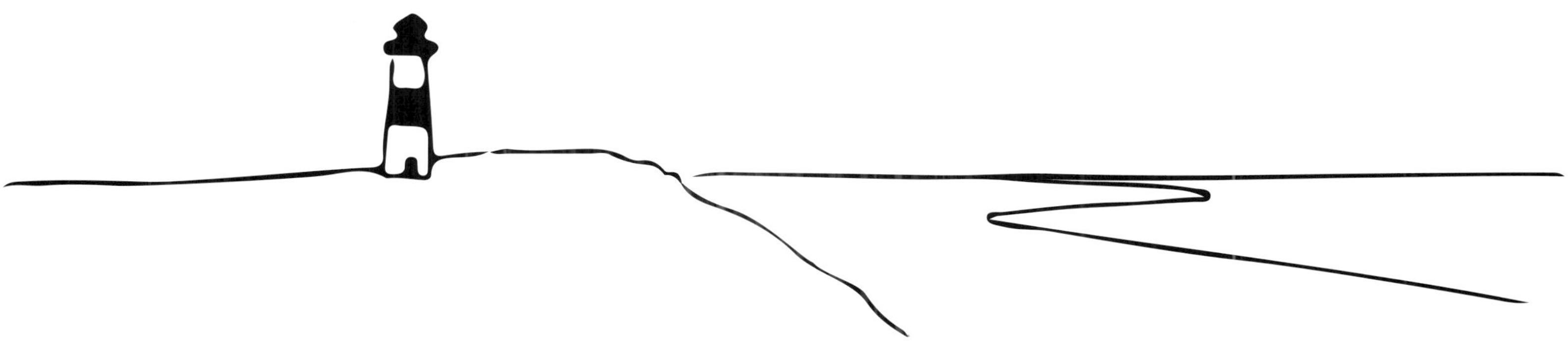

SYLT

Longing for Sylt

Der Sonnenuntergang über der Nordsee ist für viele ein Highlight.
Sunset at the North Sea is a highlight for many.

Inhalt
Content

Inhalt
Content

Man kann sich gut vorstellen, dass das Kitesurfen hier viel Spaß macht.
One can well imagine so much fun from kitesurfing here.

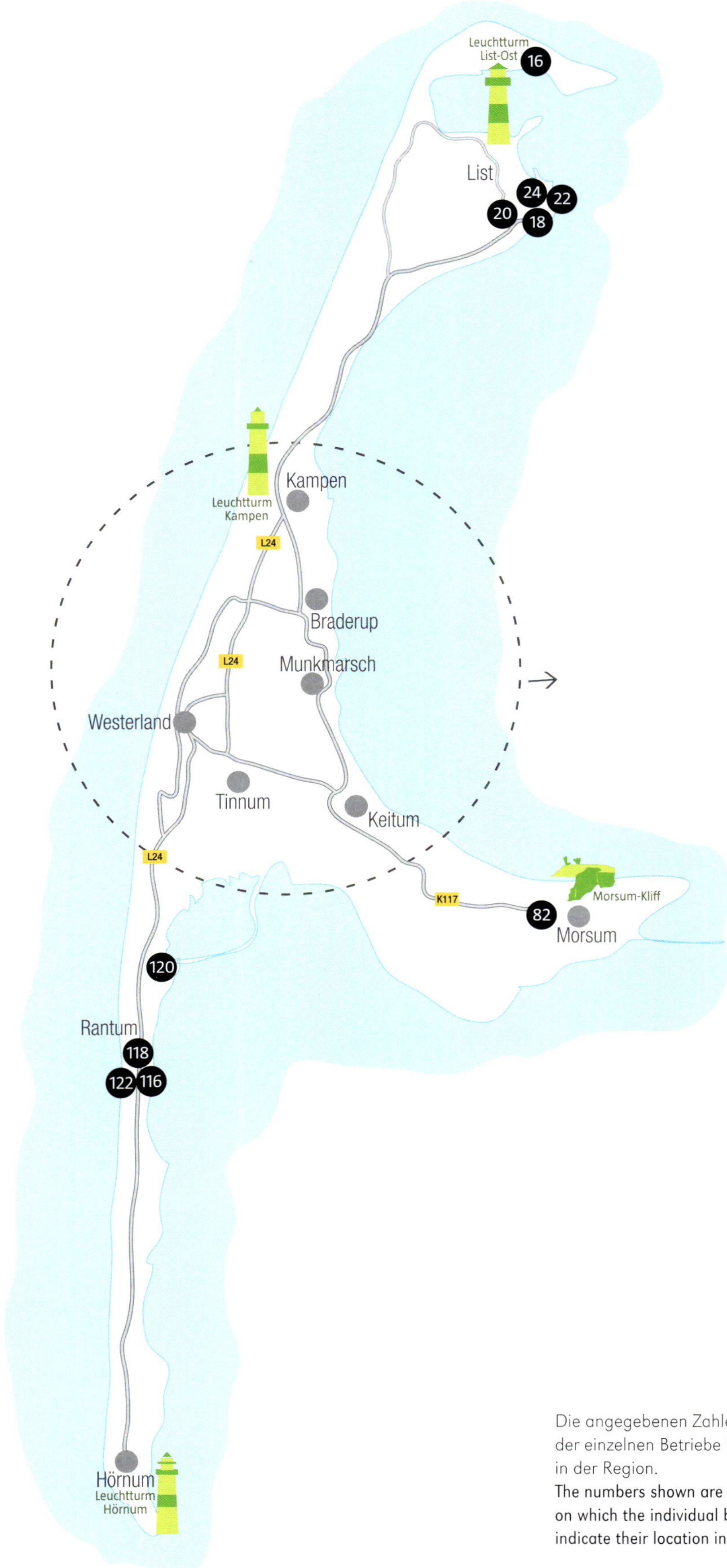

Die angegebenen Zahlen sind identisch mit den Seitenzahlen der einzelnen Betriebe in diesem Buch und bezeichnen ihre Lage in der Region.

The numbers shown are identical with the numbers of the pages on which the individual businesses are described in this book and indicate their location in the region.

Auf dem einfachsten Weg zu den spannendsten Adressen der Insel! Neben jedem Kundenporträt finden Sie einen QR-Code. Beim Einscannen dieses QR-Codes erstellt sich automatisch ein Eintrag in Ihrem Smartphone mit allen relevanten Daten wie Adresse, E-Mail, Internetadresse, Telefonnummer. Mittels eines Routenplaners lässt sich anhand dieser gespeicherten Daten eine Route über die Insel erstellen.

Get to the most exciting places on the island in the easiest possible way! Next to each customer profile you will find a QR code. When scanning this QR code you will receive an automatically generated entry in your smartphone with all the relevant data such as address, e-mail, web address, phone number. By means of a route planner and on the basis of the stored data you can generate a route over the island.

Auf Sylt weht öfter mal eine steife Brise. Dank der Strandkörbe kann man sich auch dann am Wasser sehr wohlfühlen.
Sylt often experiences a stiff breeze, but thanks to the wicker beach chairs, time spent at the water can be very enjoyable.

Urlaubsparadies Sylt

Die nordfriesische Insel Sylt: die wildeste Brandung der deutschen Nordsee an fast 40 Kilometern weißem Sandstrand, das Weltnaturerbe Schleswig-Holsteinisches Wattenmeer, steile Kliffs, unvergleichliche Dünenlandschaften, Heidegebiete mit einmaliger Flora und Fauna, sehr gute Möglichkeiten zum Baden und dazu eine stets frische Meeresbrise mit dem Duft von Meer und Watt. Facetten der Natur, die sich nirgendwo sonst in dieser Vielfalt so komprimiert erleben lassen. Diese Einmaligkeit der Natur Sylts zog schon vor über 100 Jahren Reisende und Erholungssuchende unwiderstehlich an. Das lang gestreckte, an einigen Stellen weniger als einen Kilometer breite, aber insgesamt 38 Kilometer lange Eiland wurde so schließlich von der Insel einiger Bauern und Fischer zu einem der beliebtesten Urlaubsziele Deutschlands. Und inzwischen stehen knapp 18 000 Erstwohnsitze sechs Millionen Übernachtungen pro Jahr gegenüber. Bei allen Herausforderungen, die so viele Touristen bedeuten, möchte doch heute kaum mehr ein Sylter und erst recht kein Urlauber auf das breite und hochwertige gastronomische Angebot, das gute kulturelle Programm, die vielfältigen Shoppingmöglichkeiten und die moderne Infrastruktur verzichten. Und das alles gäbe es eben nicht ohne den Tourismus, dem mit Abstand größten Wirtschaftsfaktor Sylts. Auf knapp 100 Quadratkilo-

HOLIDAY PARADISE SYLT

The North Frisian island of Sylt: the wildest surf in Germany's North Sea along almost 25 miles of white sand beaches, the World Natural Heritage Site of Schleswig-Holstein's Wadden Sea, steep cliffs, incomparable dune landscapes, heathlands with unique flora and fauna, excellent opportunities for bathing and a continual, fresh sea breeze with its smell of the North Sea and Wadden Sea as well. Facets of nature that cannot be experienced anywhere else in such diversity so close together. This unique quality of Sylt's nature had already begun to irresistibly attract travellers as well as those seeking relaxation over 100 years ago. While at some places it is less than a kilometre wide, this elongated – in total 38 kilometres long – island thus ultimately changed from an isle of a few fishermen and farmers into one of the most popular holiday destinations in Germany. And meanwhile there are almost 18,000 principal residencies compared to six million overnight stays annually. With all the challenges involved by having so many tourists, hardly any of the residents, and certainly none of the holiday makers, wish today to go without the wide range of high class gastronomic delights on offer, the good cultural programme, the diverse shopping possibilities and the modern infrastructure. And indeed, this would all not exist without the tourism, by far the largest economic factor for Sylt. On almost 100 square kilometres, Sylt offers extra-

Sylt bietet seinen Gästen vielfältige Vergnügungen. Der eine liebt es wild, der andere seicht.
Sylt offers its guests quite diverse amusements. Some like it wild, others more sedate.

metern bietet Sylt außergewöhnlich viel Abwechslung: So liegen zwischen Westerland und Keitum zwar nur knapp fünf Kilometer, mit dem Zug sind das nur wenige Minuten. Aber zwischen dem Trubel von Fußgängerzone und Promenade des Hauptortes und der beinahe absoluten Ruhe am Keitumer Wattenmeer liegen dennoch Welten. Und während an manchen Stränden zwischen Rantum und Hörnum bei ausgelassenen Strandpartys Weine für einige Hundert Euro getrunken werden, sieht der Wanderer im Marschland zwischen Morsum und Tinnum oft mehr Schafe und Kühe als Touristen. Unterschiedliche Menschen können hier also ganz verschiedene Dinge erleben und am Abend doch das Gleiche behaupten, nämlich, dass sie eine tolle Zeit gehabt hätten. Und unsere Porträts von Sylter Unternehmern und Firmen zeigen schließlich, dass neben dem Glauben an die eigene Idee und der Freude an der täglichen Arbeit immer auch die Begeisterung für den Standort Sylt von Bedeutung ist. Man ist bewusst hier und will nicht nur von der Insel leben, sondern ihr auch etwas zurückgeben, dafür sorgen, dass Sylt liebenswert bleibt und auch morgen noch ein lohnenswertes Ziel ist. Denn was die Insulaner mit den Besuchern verbindet, ist eine Leidenschaft für diese eine Insel, die „Sehnsucht Sylt".

ordinarily generous variety: Whereas between Westerland and Keitum it is hardly five kilometres – only a few minutes by train – between the hustle and bustle of the pedestrian zone and promenade of the main town, and the almost complete tranquillity of Keitum's Wadden Sea there is a truly wide gulf. And while on some beaches between Rantum and Hörnum, at exuberant parties, a few hundred euros worth of wine is being drunk, the wanderer in the marshland between Morsum and Tinnum often sees more sheep and cows than tourists. Various people can therefore experience very different things here and during the evenings they can assert the very same, and that is, that they have had a very good time. And our portraits of Sylt businesses and companies ultimately demonstrate that along with the belief in one's own idea, and the joy in one's daily work, the enthusiasm for "beach site" Sylt is always of importance as well. One is quite aware here – and does not simply live from the island, but also gives something back to it, thus ensuring that Sylt remains amiable and will still be a worthwhile destination in future as well, because that which connects the islanders with the visitors here is a passion for this particular island, known as: "Sehnsucht Sylt".

Meditative Minuten am Strand und sportliche Aktion hoch zu Ross beim Polo: Beides ist typisch Sylt.
Meditative minutes on the beach and sportive action high in the saddle, playing polo: both typical Sylt.

Sylt und die schönen Dinge ergänzen sich seit vielen Jahrzehnten.
Sylt and those lovely things complemented each other for many decades.

Bei Ebbe wirkt die Sylter Wattseite immer besonders still. – Sie brauchen auch mal etwas Ruhe? Dann nichts wie hin.
At low tide, Sylt's Wadden Sea coast always seems especially calm. Maybe you too need some peace and quiet? So, let's go.

XCEL
KITESCHULE-SYLT.DE
PHILIPP „Pile“ BRÜCKMANN
WORLD CUP RIDER
TEL: +49 (0)172 4721748

Magie und Freiheit

Die älteste und größte Kitesurf-Schule der Insel gehört Philipp Brückmann. Der in vielen Wettkämpfen erfolgreiche Surfprofi gründete 2008 seine mobile Kiteschule, und seit 2010 „parkt" er meistens an seinem Lieblingsort, am Königshafen beim Lister Ellenbogen. An dieser wunderschönen Ecke der Insel sind die Bedingungen für Anfänger ideal: flaches Wasser ohne Strömung und Wellen. Neben Kitesurfen kann hier auch Windsurfen und Stand-up-Paddling gelernt werden. Man sollte schon ein wenig sportlich sein, aber ansonsten kann hier jeder ab 30 Kilogramm Körpergewicht den Sport lernen; Brückmanns bisher ältester Schüler war sogar schon 76. Auf die Einhaltung der Sicherheitsstandards kann man sich hier natürlich ebenso verlassen wie auf die Qualität des Materials. Brückmann verwendet ausschließlich topaktuelles Equipment, und selbst in größeren Kursen bekommt jeder, sobald es geht, einen eigenen Schirm an die Hand. Sind Theorie und die ersten mühsamen Lernschritte erst mal verstanden, kommt aber auch das Erlebnis nicht zu kurz. Sicher auch ein Grund, warum über 60 Prozent der Anfänger diesem Sport treu bleiben. „Mein Ziel ist, dass die Schüler hier am Ende des Tages mit einem breiten Grinsen aus dem Wasser kommen, und das auch möglichst schon nach der ersten Lektion. Surfen bedeutet Freiheit, und dieses Lebensgefühl, diese Magie ist es, was uns Spaß macht", schwärmt Philipp Brückmann. Und er hat für jeden den richtigen Kurs parat: also schnell anmelden und rauf aufs Brett!

MAGIC AND FREEDOM

The oldest and largest kitesurfing school on the island belongs to Philipp Brückmann. Successful in many competitions, this surfing pro founded his mobile kite school in 2008, and since 2010 he usually 'parks' at his favourite location, at Königshafen Bay on List's Ellenbogen. At this beautiful corner of the island the conditions for beginners are ideal: flat waters without currents or waves. As well as kitesurfing, windsurfing and standup paddleboarding can also be learned. One should indeed be a little athletic, but otherwise anyone above 30 kilogrammes bodyweight can learn the sport; Brückmann's oldest student to date was 76 years old. Students here can of course rely on adherence to safety standards just as much as on quality of materials. Brückmann exclusively uses cutting-edge equipment, and even on larger courses every participant receives their own kite as soon as possible. Mastering the theory and the first arduous learning steps does not mean missing out on a good experience. Certainly this is one reason why over 60 percent of beginners remain with the sport. "My goal is that at the end of the day my students here come out of the water with a broad grin, and hopefully straight after the first learning session. Surfing means freedom, and it's this awareness of life, this magic that is so joyful", enthuses Philipp Brückmann, and he has the right course ready for anyone: so, register soon and get on the boards!

KITESCHULE SYLT
Philipp Brückmann
Am Ellenbogen
25992 List
Telefon 01 72 / 472 17 48
info@kiteschule-sylt.de
www.kiteschule-sylt.de

Reiche Ernte im Wattenmeer

In der Blidselbucht, südöstlich von List, wo die Nordsee besonders sauber ist, lebt die Sylter Royal, die einzige Zuchtauster Deutschlands. Mindestens zwei Jahre lang werden die Tiere von Dittmeyer's Austern-Compagnie betreut, bis sie auf den Tellern der Gourmets landen. 50 Jahre lang hatte es auf Sylt gar keine Austernfischerei mehr gegeben, die Bestände waren überfischt. Durch die Aquakultur konnte die Firma dann ab 1986 die jahrhundertelange Tradition fortsetzen, zur Freude vieler Feinschmecker. Für das Team um Bine Pöhner bedeutet das viel körperliche Arbeit, immer abhängig von Wetter und Gezeiten. Unter anderem müssen in Handarbeit die großen netzartigen Austernsäcke, die „Poches", systematisch bewegt werden. Im Sommer liegen diese auf Eisengestellen im Wattenmeer, den Winter überdauern die Austern in den großen Austernbecken der Compagnie. Durch eine eigene Meerwasserleitung gespeist dienen diese auch als Zwischenlager, um den Bedarf saisonunabhängig decken zu können. Denn die Sylter Royal ist heiß begehrt: Zwei Drittel der Produktion verlassen die Insel gut gekühlt in Richtung diverser Restaurants und Feinkostgeschäfte im In- und Ausland. Wer in Dittmeyer's gemütlichem Bistro, der Austernstube, bei einem guten Wein Austern oder andere Spezialitäten probiert, kann dabei durch Fensterscheiben den Züchtern bei der Arbeit zusehen und viel über das königliche Schalentier erfahren. Wer noch mehr wissen will, kann – nach Voranmeldung – an Austernseminaren teilnehmen.

RICH HARVEST IN WADDEN SEA

In Blidsel Bay, south-east of List, where the North Sea is especially clean, lives the Sylter Royal, the only cultivated oysters in Germany. For at least two years the little creatures are looked after by Dittmeyer's Austern-Compagnie, before they land on the plates of the gourmets. For 50 years there were no longer any oyster fisheries on Sylt, the stocks of them were overfished. Through aquaculture, the company was then able to continue the centuries-long tradition in 1986, to the joy of many connoisseurs of food. For the team of Bine Pöhner, it means much hard physical work, always dependent on the weather and the tides. Amongst other tasks, the large net-like oyster bags, known as 'poches' must be systematically manhandled and moved. In summer, these are laying on iron stands in Wadden Sea, in winter the oysters spend the season in the company's large oyster tanks. With its own saltwater system, these tanks serve also as an interim storage facility in order to cover demand independent of the season. This is due to the Sylter Royal being much sought after: Two thirds of production leave the island well cooled, on their way to various restaurants and delicatessens at home and abroad. Those who try out oysters or other specialities in Dittmeyer's cosy 'Austernstube' bistro with a glass of fine wine, can watch the oyster breeders at work through the windows, and learn much about this royal shellfish. Those who wish to find out more, can – after advance reservation – take part in oyster seminars..

AUSTERNSTUBE SYLTER ROYAL
Dittmeyer´s Austern-Compagnie GmbH
Hafenstraße 10–12
25992 List
Telefon 046 51 / 87 75 25
www.sylter-royal.de

Dittmeyer's Austern Compagnie
SYLTER
ROYAL
AUSTERN
STUBE
4025

Stressfreier Luxus in List

Das 2010 eröffnete Hotel A-ROSA Sylt am Lister Oststrand ist zu einer festen Größe auf der Insel geworden. Direktor Gordon Debus kann sich über mangelnde Nachfrage nicht beklagen: „Gerade Menschen, die im Job schon sehr viel zu organisieren haben, möchten im Urlaub nicht unbedingt weiter den Manager spielen", erklärt Debus, „sie wollen sich auf bewährte Strukturen verlassen, sich vor allem erholen, Gutes genießen, vielleicht etwas Besonderes erleben." Und da hat das A-ROSA Sylt eine Menge zu bieten: 151 luxuriös eingerichtete Zimmer, 26 Suiten, zwei Spitzenrestaurants sowie eine große Lounge mit Kamin, Bar und Livemusik. Hinzu kommt der 3500-Quadratmeter-Spa-Bereich auf zwei Ebenen inklusive Außenflächen. Überall steht den Gästen natürlich das gut geschulte Hotelpersonal zur Verfügung. Ergänzend kann aus zahlreichen Aktiv- und Sportkursen sowie weiteren Veranstaltungen ausgewählt werden. „Mit der Firma Sylt Event haben wir den Marktführer für Events um und auf Sylt direkt im Haus", freut sich Hotelchef Debus. Für Eltern, die im Familienurlaub auch mal ein paar schöne Stunden zu zweit erleben wollen, ist neben dem Babysitterservice das Kinderprogramm ideal: Das tägliche Angebot in ROSINIS Kinderklub ergänzen zum Beispiel Kinderpartys, Schwimmkurse oder geführte Ausflüge in die nahe Natur. „Wir bieten Erholung und Erlebnis für viele Zielgruppen auf sehr hohem Niveau, aber immer in ungezwungener, entspannter Atmosphäre", fasst Gordon Debus zusammen.

A-ROSA SYLT
Listlandstraße 11
25992 List
Telefon 046 51 / 967 50-0
sylt@a-rosa.de
www.a-rosa.de

STRESS-FREE LUXURY IN LIST

Hotel A-ROSA Sylt, which opened in 2010, on the Eastern List Beach has become a permanent fixture on the island. Manager Gordon Debus has no reason to complain about a lack of demand. "Especially those who have to organise so much during their working lives do not particularly wish to play the boss while they are on holiday", says Debus, "they wish to rely on well established structures, and above all to relax, and perhaps experience something special. So, here the A-ROSA Sylt hotel has much to offer: 151 luxuriously prepared rooms, 26 suites, two top restaurants as well as a large lounge with a fireplace, bar and live music. In addition, there is the 3,500 square metre spa-area on two levels including external zones. Above all the well-schooled hotel staff is of course at the service of all the guests. Furthermore, there are activities on offer as well as sports courses and other events to be chosen. "The company SyltEvent represents the market leader in events right here on and around Sylt" the hotel manager, Debus, is pleased to announce. For parents who also wish to experience a few pleasant hours alone during their family holiday there is, along with the babysitter service, the ideal children's programme: The daily offers in Rosini's Children's Club include for instance children's parties, swimming courses and accompanied excursions into the surrounding nature. "We offer relaxation and an experience for many diverse target groups at a very high level, but always in an informal, relaxed atmosphere." Gordon Debus summarises.

Das nördlichste Eis des Landes

List hat ein eindeutiges Touristenzentrum, den großen Platz am Hafen, mit der Tonnenhalle, den verschiedenen Restaurants und Geschäften. Und für Kinder und Eltern ist das Ziel noch klarer: Der Spielplatz an der Nordostspitze. Und genau dort – wie praktisch – befindet sich das Eiscafé Venezia. Es ist nicht irgendein Eis, das es hier gibt, denn Mario Hodak und seine Frau Maida tun etwas, das nicht nur auf Sylt immer seltener wird: Sie stellen über 30 Sorten und die Waffeln selbst her, und das nur aus besten Zutaten, ohne künstliche Zusätze. „Das ist die Basis unseres Erfolgs", sagt Hodak, der 2007 an diesen ganz besonderen Ort zog und gemeinsam mit Maida einen beruflichen Traum verwirklichte. Denn Mario ist Eismacher aus Leidenschaft: „Er würde am liebsten den ganzen Tag an der Eismaschine stehen", verrät seine Frau. „Es bringt aber auch Spaß, die eigenen Sorten immer noch zu verfeinern oder sich neue auszudenken", erklärt Hodak, in dessen Familie schon seit mehreren Generationen Eis hergestellt wird. Allerdings ist er der Erste der Familie, der das auf Sylt tut. Und so kann Mario nun theoretisch jederzeit aufs Meer schauen. Aber während die Gäste auf der Terrasse des Venezia den unverbaubaren Blick nach Dänemark bei Spaghettieis oder Prosecco genießen, ist der Chef schon wieder bei der Arbeit. Sonniges Wetter ist angesagt, und da können die Kunden wieder nicht genug bekommen von seinem Eis aus Tahiti-Vanilleschoten, Cookies, Piemontnüssen oder sizilianischen Pistazien.

THE NORTHERNMOST ICE CREAM IN THE COUNTRY

List has a quite obvious tourist centre, the large square by the harbour, with its old Tonnenhalle, which hosts various shops, as well as further restaurants and businesses outside. And for children and parents the objective is even more obvious: the playground on the north-east corner. It is right here too – how practical – that an ice cream parlour, the Eiscafé Venezia, is situated. It's not just any ice cream that is to be found here, what Mario Hodak and his wife Maida are doing is to ensure that on Sylt, some things will not become more seldom: They have created themselves over thirty kinds of ice cream and their wafers, using only the best ingredients, without artificial additives. "This is the basis of our success", says Hodak, who moved to this very special location in 2007, and together with Maida they realised a professional dream. Indeed, Mario is a passionate ice cream maker: "He would preferably stand at the ice cream machine all day", his wife reveals. "It is though, a lot of fun to keep improving on one's own creations and to think up new possibilities", explains Hodak, in whose family there has been ice cream manufacture for several generations. He is however the first in the family to do so on Sylt. And so, theoretically, Mario can now look out to sea at any time. Although, while the customers on Venezia's terrace enjoy the unobstructed view across to Denmark with a spaghetti ice cream or a glass of Prosecco, the manager is already back at his work. If sunny weather is to be expected, then once again the customers cannot get enough of his ice creams, flavoured with Tahiti vanilla pods, cookies, Piedmont nuts or Sicilian pistachios.

EISCAFÉ VENEZIA
Mario Hodak
Am Hafen 20
25992 List
Telefon 046 51 / 449 52 18

Weißes Gold aus List

Im Umfeld von Alexandro Pape wird es niemals langweilig. Und das Beste ist: Von den Einfällen des ehemaligen Zwei-Sterne-Kochs hat eigentlich jeder etwas, wie bei der Sylter Meersalzmanufaktur. Die Grundidee ist, edles Salz, wie das Fleur de Sel, das man aus den sogenannten Salzgärten Südeuropas kennt, aus Nordseewasser herzustellen. Die besonders gute Meerwasserqualität rund um Sylt ist ein starkes Argument, aber das nordfriesische Wetter bietet zu wenig Sonne. Am Ende einer jahrelangen Suche steht 2013 eine Entsalzungsanlage, die in dieser Form weltweit einmalig ist. Das angewendete thermische Verfahren basiert auf dem bekannten Prinzip von Verdunstung und anschließender Kondensation. Das frische Salzwasser wird über die extra verlängerte Leitung der benachbarten Sylter Austern-Compagnie aus dem Wattenmeer entnommen. Am Schluss hat man reines Meersalz und pures Wasser. Bis zu 70 Kilogramm können so täglich hergestellt werden. Das grobe Salz wird mithilfe eines speziellen Kristallisators geerntet, das Feinsalz wird abgeschöpft. Auch das Abfüllen in die typischen kleinen Gläschen und das Etikettieren geschieht in reiner Handarbeit. Beide Sorten des Sylter Meersalzes können unter anderem in dem kleinen Shop der Manufaktur probiert und gekauft werden. Passend zum Thema Salz und Kulinarik findet man hier außerdem verschiedene hochwertige Geschenkartikel. Inzwischen stellt die Manufaktur auch ihre eigenen Nudeln und eigenes Bier her, doch das ist wieder eine neue Geschichte.

WHITE GOLD FROM LIST

It is never boring in the company of Alexandro Pape, and the best part is indeed that everyone benefits from the inspirations of this former two star chef, such as from the Sylter Meersalzmanufaktur (Sylt sea-salt factory). The basic idea is to produce premium salt – such as Fleur de Sel, which one knows from the so-called salt gardens of Southern Europe – from North Sea water. The especially good quality of the sea water all around Sylt is a strong argument, although the North Frisian weather offers insufficient sunshine. At the end of years of searching, a desalination plant came into existence in 2013 which, in its existing form is unique worldwide. The adopted thermal process is based on the well-known principle of evaporation and subsequent condensation. The fresh salt water is taken out of Wadden Sea via a specially lengthened pipeline from the neighbouring Sylt Oyster Company. Finally, one is left with pure sea salt and fresh water. In this way up to 70 kilogrammes can be produced daily. The coarse salt is harvested by means of a special crystalliser and the fine salt is then separated off. Filling up the typical, small glass jars and their labelling is also carried out entirely by hand. Both types of the Sylt sea salt can, amongst other things, be tasted and purchased in the factory's small shop. In line with the topic salt and cuisine there are also various high class gift items to be found here. In the meantime the factory also produces its own noodles and its own beer, but this is however another story.

SYLTER MEERSALZMANUFAKTUR
Sylter Meersalz GmbH & Co. KG
Hafenstraße 2
25992 List
Telefon 046 51 / 942 90 74
kontakt@sylter-meersalz.de
www.sylter-meersalz.de

Verschüttete Geschichte

Wer historisch interessiert ist und die Augen offen hält, der wird sich auf Sylt schnell die eine oder andere Frage zur Inselgeschichte stellen. Immerhin wurde Sylt schon im 12. Jahrhundert erstmals urkundlich erwähnt, und selbst vor 6000 Jahren lebten hier schon Menschen. Eine ganze Reihe von Antworten findet man in den Keitumer Museen des syltfriesischen Heimatverbands Söl'ring Foriining: Im Altfriesischen Haus kann man sehr lebensnah nachvollziehen, wie der Alltag vor über 200 Jahren aussah. Und das Sylter Heimatmuseum betrachtet von den Anfängen bis in die jüngere Zeit erstaunlich vielfältige Aspekte der Inselgeschichte. So kann der Besucher neben archäologischen Funden beispielsweise auch viel Kunst zum Thema Sylt betrachten, die Webtechnik der einst bedeutenden Sylter Textilproduktion nachvollziehen oder einige Minuten in der rekonstruierten ehemaligen Kampener Künstlerkneipe Ziegenstall verbringen. Der Söl'ring Foriining e.V. betreut auch noch zwei weitere historische Stätten: Im außergewöhnlich gut erhaltenen Großsteingrab Denghoog in Wenningstedt kann man sich in Sylts steinzeitliche Periode vor etwa 5000 Jahren zurückversetzen, und in der Kampener Vogelkoje über die bis Anfang des 20. Jahrhunderts übliche Praxis des Vogelfangs informieren. Im Süden von Westerland betreibt außerdem der Jägerverein Hegering Sylt noch die

SUBMERGED HISTORY

Those visitors interested in history and who keep their eyes open will soon have one or two questions about Sylt and the island's history. After all, Sylt was first mentioned in a document in the 12th century, and as long as 6,000 years ago there were already people living here. A whole series of answers can be found in Keitum's museums of the Sylt-Frisian homeland traditions association Söl'ring Forrining: In the old-Frisian house one can very realistically comprehend what daily life looked like over 200 years ago. And Sylt's homeland traditions museum considers astoundingly diverse aspects of island life from its beginnings up to modern times. Along with archaeological finds, the visitor can thus for instance see many art exhibits connected with Sylt, retrace the weaving techniques of the once influential Sylt textile production or spend a few minutes in the reconstructed former Ziegenstall artists' pub in Kampen. The Söl'ring Foriining association also maintains two further historical sites: In the unusually well preserved Denghoog megalithic tomb in Wenningstedt one can think back to Sylt's Stone Age era about 5,000 years ago, and hear about the practice, common into the twentieth century, of bird catching in Kampen's Vogelkoje (bird sanctuary). In addition, in the South of Westerland the Jägerverein Hegering Sylt runs the Vogelkoje Eidum. Eidum was once the name of the former Westerland, which was situated west of

Spannende Einblicke in die Vergangenheit: Sylter Heimatmuseum (links) und Großsteingrab Denghoog.
Fascinating insights into the past : Sylt's local heritage museum (left) and Denghoog megalithic tomb.

St. Severin in Keitum: Jahrhundertelang half sie nicht nur Gläubigen, sondern auch der Schifffahrt bei der Orientierung.
For centuries St. Severin in Keitum has not only assisted believers but also in the navigation of ships at sea.

Militärische Relikte: die „Seekühe" im Lister Wattenmeer. Heute willkommene Abwechslung für Vögel und Touristenblicke.
Military relics: The 'sea cows' in List's Wadden Sea. Today, a welcome change for birds and the gaze of tourists.

Vogelkoje Eidum. Eidum war auch der Name des Vorgängers Westerlands, der westlich der heutigen Küste lag und im 15. Jahrhundert infolge zahlreicher Sturmfluten endgültig aufgegeben wurde. Ähnliche Schicksale trafen auch ehemalige Ortschaften wie Alt-Rantum, Stedum oder Alt-List. Manche Siedlungen wurde zudem nach und nach von Wanderdünen verschüttet. Sylt ist auch aus diesem Grunde ein interessanter Ort für Archäologen. Relikte des Zweiten Weltkriegs sind die skurril wirkenden „Seekühe" in der Blidselbucht südlich von List: Die Betongerüste dienten der Luftwaffe einst als Zielscheiben. Auch das Rantumbecken stammt aus dieser Zeit: 1936/37 wurde ein Teil des Wattenmeeres auf 5,2 Kilometern eingedeicht, um eine Landefläche für Wasserflugzeuge zu erhalten, was sich in der Praxis jedoch nicht bewährte. Seit 1962 wird das Rantumbecken als Seevogelschutzgebiet genutzt. So manche Träne schließlich floss 1970 bei der endgültigen Einstellung der Sylter Inselbahn. Sie hatte seit 1888 auf verschiedenen Strecken ihren Dienst getan, war aber nun gegenüber Autos und Bussen nicht mehr konkurrenzfähig. Ihre letzten beiden Achsen finden sich heute als Denkmal vor dem Fernbahnhof Westerland. Soweit nur einige der zahlreichen Geschichten aus der Sylter Vergangenheit. Wer noch mehr wissen will, kann überall auf Sylt leicht fündig werden.

today's coastline and was finally given up due to many 15th century storm floods. Similar fates were experienced by other former locations such as Alt-Rantum, Stedum and Alt-List. Some settlements were furthermore submerged step by step by wandering dunes. Sylt is for this reason also an interesting place for archaeologists. The bizzare 'sea cows' in Blidsel Bay are WWII relics south of List: The concrete frames served as targets for the Luftwaffe. Rantum Basin also originates from this time: In 1936/37 a 5.2 kilometre stretch of Wadden Sea was diked to create a landing zone for seaplanes, which proved impractical in practice. Rantum Basin has been a seabird conservation area since 1962. A few tears were ultimately shed in 1970 during the final cessation of Sylt's island railway. It was in service on various stretches since 1888, but could no longer compete with cars and buses. Its last two axles are a monument in front of Westerland's long distance railway station.
Here then, just a few of the many stories from Sylt's rich past. Those who wish to find out more will easily discover much in addition everywhere around the island.

Sylts Nordspitze: Die Brandung ist hier oft besonders wild (links). Der Radweg nach List folgt der ehemaligen Bahntrasse.
Sylt's northern point: The surf here is often quite wild (left). The cycling track to List is on the route of the former railway line.

Der Luxus echten Handwerks

Ohne die Bäckerei & Konditorei Speck würde Kampen viel fehlen. Sie repräsentiert – im besten Sinne – ein Stück Sylt, wie es früher war. Holger Speck wurde hier geboren und führt den Familienbetrieb nun in dritter Generation. Genau wie schon 1950 bei seinem Großvater werden die Backwaren hier ganz ohne Fertigmischungen oder Zusatzsstoffe von Hand hergestellt. Meister Speck und sein kleines Team backen überwiegend nach Familienrezepten und ausschließlich in der eigenen Backstube, die seit dem Umzug in das neue Haus 1986 nun direkt neben dem kleinen Laden liegt. „Leider greifen immer mehr Bäcker auf Backmischungen oder vorgefertigte Rohlinge zurück", erzählt Holger Speck. Das sei auch ein Grund, warum die Brötchen inzwischen fast überall gleich schmeckten. Zumindest seine eigenen Kunden kann der Bäckermeister aber beruhigen: „Für mich kommt das nicht in Frage: Mir macht die traditionelle Handwerksarbeit Spaß, und ich weiß ja auch, was die Leute mögen." Specks Angebot von derzeit 27 Brötchen- und acht Brotsorten sowie einer großen Auswahl an Keksen, Kuchen und Torten ist nicht nur in Kampen sehr beliebt. Auch aus anderen Orten der Insel kommen täglich viele Sylter und Urlauber, um bei Speck einzukaufen. Immerhin, die Keitumer haben seit 2013 das Glück, seine einzige Filiale im Ort zu haben. Speck ist ein Stück lebendiges Sylt und will es auch gern bleiben: „Ich freue mich darüber, wenn ich alle paar Tage höre: ‚Ihre Brötchen schmecken wirklich noch so lecker wie früher!'"

THE LUXURY OF TRUE CRAFTSMANSHIP

Without the Speck's bakery and pastry shop in Kampen there would truly be a lot missing. It represents – in the best sense – a piece of Sylt as it once was. Holger Speck was born here and he now runs this family business in its third generation. Just as in his grandfather's day back in 1950, all bakery goods are produced by hand quite without any ready-mixed ingredients or additives. Master Speck and his small team bake largely according to family recipes and exclusively in their own bakery which, since the relocation into their new house in 1986 is now directly beside their small shop. "Unfortunately, there is a growing number of bakers who resort to using ready-mixed ingredients or pre-processed pastry shells", says Holger Speck. This is probably also one reason why meanwhile bread rolls taste the same no matter where you are. At least the master baker can reassure his own customers: "For me there is no question about it: I find much pleasure in using traditional craftsmanship, and I also know what my customers desire." Mr Speck's current range of 27 different types of bread roll and 8 types of bread, as well as a large selection of biscuits, cakes and gâteaux create high demand and not only in Kampen: From other locations on the island, many Sylt natives and holidaymakers arrive daily in order to make their purchases at Speck's. Although now too, the residents of Keitum are lucky enough to have Speck's only branch shop since 2013. Mr Speck is a living piece of Sylt and wishes to keep it that way: "It makes me very happy when every few days I hear: "Your bread rolls really do still taste just as nice as they used to!"

BÄCKEREI & KONDITOREI SPECK
Inhaber: Holger Speck
Süderweg 1
25999 Kampen
Telefon 046 51 / 425 60
speck-baeckerei@web.de
www.baeckerei-speck.de

Mit goldenen Grüßen

Eine kostbare Uhr oder ein wertvoller Ring ist keine Ware, die man nach kurzer Ansicht mal eben so mitnimmt. Niemand weiß das besser als Torsten H. Spliedt, der in der fünften Generation das Familienunternehmen heute in Kampen auf Sylt leitet. Der Ursprung der Juweliere Spliedt wurde damals vor 150 Jahren in Itzehoe gelegt. Das Geschäft existiert seit weit mehr als zehn Jahren in dem exklusiven Ferienort Kampen auf Sylt. Hier werden feine Chronometer aus der Schweiz und edle bis einzigartige Schmuckstücke aus deutschen Manufakturen gezeigt. Juwelier Spliedt und seine Mitarbeiter beraten ihre Kunden in angenehmer Atmosphäre. Da setzt man sich auch schon mal zusammen in den Strandkorb vor dem Geschäft, unterhält sich in aller Ruhe und versucht gemeinsam, das richtige, das eine Stück zu finden. Dies wissen auch die Kunden beim Juwelier Spliedt besonders zu schätzen, die entspannte und kompetente Beratung und die hohe Qualität der Produkte. Aktuell entsteht ein neuer Standort in Hamburg, Neue ABC-Str.4, der diese hohe Qualität der Beratung und die entspannte Atmosphäre von Sylt nach Hamburg bringen wird.

WITH GOLDEN GREETINGS

A valuable watch or a precious ring is not something one decides upon after only a brief look. Nobody knows this better than Torsten H. Spliedt who today runs the family business in its fifth generation in Kampen on Sylt. The origins of the Spliedt jewellers have their roots over 150 years ago in Itzehoe. Today's business exists for well over 10 years in the exclusive holiday resort of Kampen on Sylt. Fine chronometers from Switzerland and elegant as well as unique pieces of jewellery by German manufacturers are presented here. Juwelier Spliedt and his staff advise thier clients in a pleasant atmosphere, perhaps sitting down together in the wicker beach chair in front of the premises, collectively conversing calmly and attempting to find that one precise, definitive piece, and the clients of Juwelier Spliedt particularly appreciate this, as well as the relaxed and competent advice and the high quality of the products. A new branch is currently being formed at Neue ABC-Str.4 in Hamburg, so the high quality of Spliedt advice on Sylt including the relaxed atmosphere there will be reproduced in Hamburg as well.

JUWELIER H. SPLIEDT SYLT GMBH
Torsten H. Spliedt
Hauptstraße 15
25999 Kampen
Telefon 046 51 / 410 01
info@spliedt-sylt.de
www.spliedt-sylt.de

Der schöne Traum der Galeristen

Träume können wahr werden. Wer das bezweifelt, kennt wahrscheinlich die Geschichte der Galerie Herold auf Sylt nicht, eines Familienunternehmens, das 2016 sein 20-jähriges Jubiläum feierte. Rainer Herold hatte viele Jahre erfolgreich in der Werbebranche gearbeitet, als er sich mit 30 Jahren entschloss, sein Hobby zum Beruf zu machen. Er spezialisierte sich auf norddeutsche Kunst der Zeit von 1870 bis 1950 und eröffnete – unter anderem mit Bildern, die er privat gesammelt hatte – 1978 seine erste Galerie in Hamburg. Der Autodidakt Herold machte sich in den folgenden Jahren einen Namen als Kunsthändler und Experte; außerdem veröffentlichte er eine ganze Reihe erfolgreicher Bücher. Seit 2005 befindet sich das Hamburger Stammhaus in den Colonnaden 5. Doch eigentlich ist Sylt die Heimat der Familie. Rainer Herold war hier gemeinsam mit seinen Brüdern aufgewachsen und verbrachte auch danach immer wieder gern Zeit auf seiner Lieblingsinsel. Aber erst Freunde brachten ihn im Sommer 1996 auf die Idee, in Kampen eine Filiale zu eröffnen. Die Sommerzeit ist traditionell eine Saure-Gurken-Zeit für Galerien, warum dann nicht den Kunden hinterherreisen? Herold mietete also kurz entschlossen einige Räume am Kampener Dorfkrug und verkaufte bereits am Eröffnungstag sein erstes Bild auf Sylt. Im Jahr 2000 zog Herold dann in den Braderuper Weg 4 um. In den schönen Räumen des Hauses Meeresruh präsentiert er nun unter anderem hochkarätige Werke von Künstlern wie Emil Nolde, Ernst Ludwig Kirchner, Erich Heckel, Max Lieber-

THE BEAUTIFUL DREAM OF THE GALLERISTS

Dreams can come true. Those that doubt it, probably don't know the story of Galerie Herold on Sylt, a family business that on the occasion of its 20th anniversary celebrated in 2016. Rainer Herold had worked successfully in the advertising industry for many years when at thirty years of age he decided to turn his hobby into his profession. He specialised in Northern German art in the period between 1870 and 1950, and in 1978 opened – with pictures, among which were some he had privately collected – his first gallery in Hamburg. Self-taught, Herold made a name for himself during the following years as an art dealer and expert. In addition, he published a whole series of successful books. The main gallery has been situated at Colonnaden 5, Hamburg since 2005. However, Sylt is the real home of his family. Rainer Herold grew up here together with his brothers, and thereafter was often pleased to spend time on his favourite island. Although, it was initially friends in the summer of 1996 who suggested to him the idea of opening a branch gallery in Kampen. Summertime is traditionally somewhat of a silly season for gallerists, so why not follow the customers on their travels? Herold thus spontaneously rented some rooms at the Dorfkrug tavern in Kampen and had already sold his first picture on Sylt on the opening day. In 2000, Herold then moved into Braderuper Weg 4. In the beautiful rooms of the Meeresruh building he now began to present, among others, high-class works by artists such as Emil Nolde, Ernst Ludwig Kirchner, Erich Heckel, Max Liebermann, Ivo Hauptmann, Otto Modersohn and Max Pechstein. Everyone was glad to call in: passers-by

Haus Meeresruh
GALERIE HEROLD
HAMBURG · KAMPEN
NORDDEUTSCHE KUNST

mann, Ivo Hauptmann, Otto Modersohn oder Max Pechstein. Alle kommen gern vorbei: kunstinteressierte Passanten, versierte Sammler sowie Leute, die eine attraktive Geldanlage suchen oder ihre Wohnung mit hochwertiger Kunst verschönern wollen. Auch viel überregionales und internationales Kunstpublikum wurde in den letzten Jahren auf diese Galerie der Klassischen Moderne in Kampen aufmerksam. Inzwischen gibt es drei Galerien Herold auf Sylt. Im Nebengebäude eröffnete 2015 Herolds Sohn Patrick eine eigene Dependance. Patrick Herold, der auch in Hamburg als Kunsthändler aktiv ist, zeigt in seiner Contemporary-Galerie zum Beispiel zeitgenössische deutsche und internationale Künstler wie Rainer Fetting, Dieter Glasmacher, Frank Schult, Markus Lüpertz und Christo. Patricks Schwester Katharina Marie betreibt seit 2014 ihre eigene Galerie in der Bahnhofstraße 4 in Keitum. In dem alten Friesenhaus präsentiert die studierte Kunsthistorikerin vor allem Werke der norddeutschen Klassischen Moderne, darunter viele Sylter Künstler wie Hugo Köcke, Hans-Peter Feddersen, Franz Korwan, Magnus Weidemann oder Bleicke Bleicken. Zusätzlich zeigt sie hier ausgewählte Keramik und Antiquitäten sowie – unter dem Label Heroldian Jewellery – von ihr selbst gefertigten Schmuck. Das Leben der beliebten Sylter Galeristen bleibt also in Bewegung. Wer noch mehr wissen will, dem sei der 2016 erschienene Jubiläumsband über die Galerie Herold auf Sylt ans Herz gelegt.

interested in art, experienced collectors, as well as people seeking an attractive investment or looking to embellish their apartment with high value art. In these last few years much of the national and international art public also became aware of this gallery of classical modernism in Kampen. Meanwhile, there are three Herold Galleries on Sylt. In the neighbouring building Herold's son Patrick opened his own branch in 2015. Patrick Herold is also an active art dealer in Hamburg. In his Contemporary Gallery for instance, he exhibits contemporary German and international artists such as Rainer Fetting, Dieter Glasmacher, Frank Schult, Markus Lüpertz and Christo. Patrick's sister Katharina Marie runs her own gallery in Bahnhofstraße 4 in Keitum since 2014. In this old Frisian house the learned art historian exhibits above all works of Northern German classical modernism, among these are many Sylt artists such as Hugo Köcke, Hans-Peter Feddersen, Franz Korwan, Magnus Weidemann and Bleicke Bleicken. In addition, she exhibits selected ceramics and antiques here as well as jewellery made by herself under the Heroldian Jewellery label. The life of the much admired Sylt gallerists thus remains in motion. For those who wish to know more, we warmly recommend the anniversary publication about Galerie Herold on Sylt which appeared in 2016.

GALERIE HEROLD
Braderuper Weg 4
25999 Kampen
Telefon: 046 51 / 451 35
herold@galerie-herold.de
www.galerie-herold.de

GALERIE HEROLD
Bahnhofstraße 4
25980 Sylt / OT Keitum
Telefon 046 51 / 446 55 50
katharina@galerie-herold.de
www.galerie-herold.de

Vom Zauber des Privaten

Das Village liegt in einer zentralen, aber ruhigen Ecke Kampens, hinter hohen Rosenhecken, fast wie ein privates Anwesen. Dennoch ist es ein kleines privates Luxushotel, geführt von den Inhabern Peter M. und Minka Stütz. Wahr ist jedoch, dass sich die Gäste hier meist besonders schnell zu Hause fühlen, allerdings mit dem Unterschied, dass vieles, was in den eigenen vier Wänden selbst gemacht werden muss, hier mit leichter Hand durch das engagierte Team des Hauses erledigt wird. Seit dem letzten Umbau 2013 ist jedes der drei Zimmer und jede der sieben Suiten neu sowie jeweils unterschiedlich gestaltet worden. Je nach Verfügbarkeit können die Räume nun auch variabel miteinander kombiniert werden. Gerade sehr anspruchsvolle Gäste, die auch im Hotel nicht auf eine individuelle geschmackvolle Einrichtung verzichten möchten, sind im Village richtig. Manche Stammgäste wollen sogar bei jedem Aufenthalt eine andere Suite ausprobieren, um immer neue Wohnerlebnisse zu haben. Solch einzigartige Raumgestaltung erfordert Erfahrung und Geschick. Das Village konnte nur mit Minka und Peter M. Stütz das werden, was es heute ist, denn die beiden sind seit vielen Jahren als exklusive Einrichtungsberater erfolgreich. Wer mehr wissen möchte, kann einen Termin im ebenso ungewöhnlichen wie verführerischen Showroom Hüs bi Hüs in Keitum vereinbaren. Das Ehepaar Stütz hat mit dem Village seine ganz persönliche Vorstellung eines idealen Hotels verwirklicht. Schöne Möbel und geschmackvolles Ambiente sind dabei allerdings nur ein Aspekt. Das ganze Village-Team will vor allem ebenso perfekter

A KIND OF MAGIC IN THE PRIVATE SPHERE

'Village' is situated in a central but peaceful corner of Kampen, behind high rose hedges, almost like a private house. It is however a small private luxury hotel, run by the owners Minka and Peter M. Stütz. It is true though, that the majority of guests here very soon feel quite at home, but nevertheless with the difference that much within one's own four walls needs to be self-made, although here it is done with a light touch by the property's own, dedicated team. Since the last reconstruction in 2013, each of the three rooms and each of the seven suites are new as well as all being individually designed. Depending on availability, the rooms and spaces can now be variably combined with one another. Particularly very demanding guests who, also in a hotel, do not wish to forgo individual tasteful decoration, are at the right place here in Village. Some regular guests even wish to try out a different suite at each visit in order to have a new living experience every time. Such unique interior design requires experience and skill. Village could only have become that which it is today through Minka and Peter M. Stütz, because the couple have been successful advisors for exclusive decoration and furnishings for many years. Anyone who wishes to find out more can arrange an appointment at the equally exceptional and seductive showroom Hüs bi Hüs in Keitum. The Village is the realisation by the married couple, Stütz, of their wholly personal vision of an ideal hotel. Beautiful furniture and tasteful ambience are however only one aspect. The whole team in Village desire above all to be the perfect and discreet host as well. Although the hotel is small, it offers more than some considerably larger hotels:

VILLAGE

wie dezenter Gastgeber sein. Obwohl das Hotel klein ist, bietet es doch mehr als manche deutlich größeren Häuser: einen hauseigenen Wellnessbereich mit Pool sowie Massage- und Fitness-Optionen, einen großen Lobbybereich mit Hotelbar, Kamin und Sonnenterrasse, jeden Nachmittag frisches hausgemachtes Gebäck sowie selbstverständlich ein reichhaltiges Frühstück mit kalten und warmen Speisen bis in die Mittagsstunden. Jeder, der im Village bucht, erhält außerdem einen kleinen, Wunschzettel genannten Fragebogen, mit dessen Hilfe der Aufenthalt bereits im Vorfeld noch individueller und angenehmer geplant werden kann. Die Vorschläge reichen von der Abholung am Flughafen oder Bahnhof über das Abklären eventueller Allergien bis zu der Möglichkeit, Tickets, Restaurantplätze oder Trainingsstunden vorab buchen zu lassen. Auch andere besondere Wünsche werden gern erfüllt. Eine nicht alltägliche Spezialität des Hauses ist außerdem das Private Dining, bei dem – nach Voranmeldung – der Koch des Hauses ein persönliches Abendessen ganz nach Wunsch in der Lobby serviert. Die eigentliche Seele des Village ist aber vor allem der familiäre und dennoch immer sensible Umgang mit dem Gast. Er kann sich auf das hoch qualifizierte und motivierte Team absolut verlassen. Die Privatsphäre unbedingt zu respektieren und dabei doch jeden Gast individuell zu betreuen, das ist die gelebte Philosophie im Village.

the property's own wellness area with a pool as well as massage and fitness options, a large lobby area with hotel bar, open fire and sun terrace. Every afternoon, freshly baked home-made pastries are served, as well as of course a comprehensive daily breakfast selection which includes cold or warm meals available right up to midday. Everyone who books into Village receives in addition a small wish list, a questionnaire with which, before arrival, the stay in the hotel may be more agreeably planned and made more individual. Suggestions range from pick-up at the airport or station to clarifying possible allergies, to the opportunity of having tickets or restaurant tables or training sessions booked in advance. Other special wishes are also gladly fulfilled. In addition, one speciality of the house is not an everyday event, but by prior arrangement it is possible to enjoy private dining, whereby the in-house chef serves a personal evening dinner in the lobby entirely as desired. The actual soul of Village is above all however the homely and nevertheless always sensitive interaction with the guests. They can absolutely rely on the highly qualified and motivated team. Implicitly respecting their personal privacy and at the same time however ensuring that they are individually looked after, this is the philosophy lived up to in Village.

VILLAGE HOTELBETRIEBS-GESELLSCHAFT MBH
Peter M. und Minka Stütz
Alte Dorfstraße 7
25999 Kampen
Telefon 046 51 / 46 97-0
hotel@village-kampen.de
www.village-kampen.de

Was kann der Mensch da mehr als staunen, fühlen, genießen? Die wilde Schönheit des Meeres bleibt schwer zu beschreiben.
Can anyone do any more than be amazed, feel emotions, enjoy the moments? The wild beauty of the sea is always difficult to describe.

Individualität als Prinzip

Seit Mitte der Achtzigerjahre gibt es in Kampen den Laden von Schmuckdesignerin Susanna Dünne. Die gebürtige Schweizerin macht hier in der Werkstatt ihr ganz eigenes Ding und am besten ständig etwas Neues und Ausgeflipptes. So kombiniert sie den Schmuck aus Gold, Platin und Edelsteinen zum Beispiel gern mit ungewöhnlichen Materialien wie Mammut-Elfenbein oder Knochenersatz. Es sind nicht zwangsläufig Einzelstücke, aber Dünne und ihr kleines Designerteam produzieren nie in Serie. Denn nach wenigen Exemplaren langweilt sie auch das schönste Objekt und eine neue kreative Idee muss her. Was aber immer zu erkennen bleibt, ist die typische Dünne-Handschrift. Dass Susanna Dünne trotz ihres enormen Outputs nur selten Lagerprobleme bekommt, verdankt sie ihrem treuen Publikum, das ihr einzigartiges Schmuckdesign regelrecht liebt. „Die rennen mir hier manchmal echt die Bude ein", erzählt Dünne lachend, „selbst in der Nebensaison ist immer was los. Neulich haben die Kolleginnen sogar meine eigene Kette verkauft, ich hatte sie eigentlich nur kurz beiseitegelegt." Aber das ist nichts, was die Designerin lange stören würde. „Ich freue mich immer, wenn jemand das perfekte Schmuckstück bei uns findet. Das passiert nicht dauernd, aber wenn, dann spüren es alle. Eine Frau wird dann plötzlich noch schöner, glücklicher und zufriedener." – Das sind die Momente, die Susanna Dünne besonders Spaß machen, und deshalb bleibt sie auch weiterhin auf der Suche nach immer neuen Ideen.

INDIVIDUALITY AS A PRINCIPLE

Jewellery designer Susanna Dünne has had her shop in Kampen since the mid-eighties. Swiss by birth, she does quite her own thing here in her studio and preferably always something new and flipped out. So she happily combines her jewellery creations of gold, platinum and gemstones with for instance unusual materials such as mammoth ivory or bone substitutes. They are not necessarily individual items, but Dünne and her small designer team never produce in series. This is because after only a few specimens even the most beautiful objects begin to bore her, and a new creative idea must be thought up. That which can always be recognised is however the typical Dünne touch. The fact that, despite Susanna Dünne's enormous output, she only seldom has problems of storage space, is thanks to her loyal clientele that truly loves her unique jewellery design. "They literally beat the proverbial path to my door here sometimes", recounts Dünne, smiling, "even in the low season there's always plenty going on. Recently, my colleagues even sold my own necklace, and I had actually only put it to one side for a moment." But this is nothing that would annoy the designer for long. "I am always pleased when someone finds the perfect piece of jewellery here. This doesn't happen all the time, but when it does then everyone notices. A woman is then suddenly more beautiful, happier and more contented." – These are the moments that are particularly pleasing for Susanna Dünne, and therefore she continues searching for ever more new ideas.

DÜNNE KAMPEN
Westerweg 14
25999 Kampen
Telefon 046 51 / 434 83
duenne-kampen@web.de
www.duenne-kampen.de

ICH TAPPE...
jedenfalls NICHT im Dunklen!

Erfahrung mit Genuss

Die meisten Gäste, die auf der sonnigen Terrasse des Hotels Walter's Hof in Kampen den einzigartigen Ausblick über Sylt genießen, ahnen wohl kaum, dass sie diese Augenblicke eigentlich schlechtem Wetter zu verdanken haben. Denn der Regen hatte tatsächlich Anteil daran, dass Detlef Tappe zum Gastgeber dieses Hotels wurde: „Ende der Siebzigerjahre machte ich Urlaub in Dänemark", erinnert sich der Hotelier, „aber es brachte alles keinen Spaß, es regnete jeden Tag, das Essen war schlecht, mein Buch langweilig. Also brach ich den Urlaub ab und fuhr mit dem Auto über Tondern zurück nach Deutschland. Da trat endlich wieder ein Sonnenstrahl aus den Wolken und fiel auf ein Schild: ‚Sylt-Shuttle'. Ich machte mich spontan auf den Weg und führte meinen Urlaub auf Sylt fort. Ich war wirklich begeistert, ergänzt Tappe, „die Luft, die Gerüche, das Meer ..." – Und so kehrte er schon bald wieder zurück nach Sylt und blieb bis heute. Das Detlef Tappes Entscheidung richtig war, ist offensichtlich: Über mangelnde Nachfrage kann sich der Hotelier, der das Hotel Walter's Hof seit 1984 führt, jedenfalls nicht beklagen. Die großzügig und individuell eingerichteten Räumlichkeiten des Hauses sind sehr beliebt, insbesondere bei Gästen, die auch im Urlaub ein bisschen mehr Platz wollen. Kein Appartement und keine Suite ist hier kleiner als 35 Quadratmeter. Wer noch mehr Raum braucht, findet mehrere exklusive Ferienwohnungen und Ferienhäuser im Angebot des Hotels Walter's Hof. Auch dort kann natürlich auf Wunsch der Hotelservice ganz oder teilweise genutzt wer-

EXPERIENCE WITH ENJOYMENT

The majority of guests who enjoy the unique view across Sylt from the sunny terrace of Hotel Walter's Hof in Kampen, would hardly realise that they actually have bad weather to thank for these moments. Indeed, it was the rain that played a part in making Detlef Tappe the host in this hotel: "At the end of the seventies I took a holiday in Denmark", the hotelier recalls, "but it was all simply no fun, it rained every day, the food was of poor quality, even my book was boring. So I broke off my holiday and drove via Tondern with the car back to Germany. There was then finally a ray of sunshine poking through the cloud cover and it fell on a road sign: 'Sylt-Shuttle'. On the spur of the moment I set off down the road and continued my holiday on Sylt. I was truly amazed", Tappe adds, "the air, the smells, the sea ..." – and he therefore returned to Sylt soon thereafter and remained to this day. That Detlef Tappe's decision was correct is quite apparent: Regarding a lack of demand: the hotelier, who has been running Hotel Walter's Hof since 1984, has in any case nothing to grumble about. The generous and individually furnished rooms and spaces within the building are very popular, especially with guests who, when on holiday too, prefer a little more space. None of the apartments or suites here are smaller than 35 square metres. But those who desire more space will find several exclusive holiday apartments and holiday homes to choose from among those on offer within the Hotel Walter's Hof programme, and even here, where desired, the hotel's services can partly or entirely be requested. The top restaurant Tappe's in Walter's Hof, the hotel

den. Das Toprestaurant Tappe's im Walter's Hof, die Hotelbar und ein Wellnessbereich runden das Angebot des Hauses ab. Die Gäste aus dem In- und Ausland schätzen vor allem den authentischen Charme und unkomplizierten Service des Hotels. „Hier ist jeder willkommen", betont Detlef Tappe, „egal, woher er kommt, egal, wie dick seine Brieftasche ist und egal, wie alt er ist". Weil auch Familien mit Kindern hier gern gesehen sind, werden auch schon mal mehrere Generationen einer Familie zu Stammgästen. „Hier haben so manche geheiratet, die als Kind hier im Hause Urlaub gemacht haben", freut sich der Hotelier. Aber nicht nur die klassischen Urlaubsgäste oder Geschäftsreisenden schätzen Walter's Hof und die vielseitigen Erfahrungen des Chefs. Denn Event-Profi Detlef Tappe hat seit Jahren viel Erfolg mit der Organisation exklusiver Veranstaltungen, die das Inselleben insgesamt deutlich bereichert haben: Das Internationale Gourmet-Festival Sylt oder das German Polo Masters in Keitum sind hierfür zwei Beispiele. Ganz gleich, was Detlef Tappe noch alles einfallen wird, eines wird er niemals toppen: die unvergleichliche Aussicht vom Hotel über die Insel. Hier, vom leicht erhöhten Standpunkt aus, kann der Blick ganz ungehindert schweifen: über Weststrand, Heide, Dünen und Wattenmeer. Vom Sonnenaufgang bis zum Sonnenuntergang ist alles hautnah erlebbar, hier im Walter's Hof in Kampen.

bar and a wellness area rounds off the facilities offered by the hotel. The guests, from home and abroad, appreciate above all the hotel's authentic charm and uncomplicated service. "Everyone is welcome here", Detlef Tappe emphasises, "no matter where he or she comes from, no matter how large or small their wallet is, nor how old he or she is". Since families with children are gladly received here, sometimes even several generations of one family become regular guests. "Some guests have married here, because they were here as children on holiday", the hotelier is pleased to admit. However, it is not only the traditional holiday guests or business travellers who appreciate Walter's Hof and the many, varied experiences of the manager. Event pro, Detlef Tappe, has had many years of success in the organisation of exclusive functions that have on the whole significantly enriched life on the island: This is exemplified by the Internationale Gourmet-Festival Sylt or the German Polo Masters in Keitum, to mention only two examples. No matter what Detlef Tappe comes up with in future, there is one thing he will never be able to beat: the incomparable view from the hotel across the island. Here, from its slightly raised position, one's unimpeded gaze can clearly scan back and forth: across Weststrand, heath, dunes and Wadden Sea. From sunrise to sunset, everything can be experienced at first hand, here in Walter's Hof in Kampen.

HOTEL WALTER'S HOF
Detlef Tappe
Kurhausstraße 23
25999 Kampen
Telefon 046 51 / 989 60
post@walters-hof.de
www.walters-hof.de

PPE´S
m Walter´s Hof

SHOES & BAGS
BARBARA LOHMANN
Cashmere
BARBARA LOHMANN

Die Schatzkästchen des Herrn K.

Dass ein Kauferlebnis glücklich machen kann, werden viele Menschen nachvollziehen können. Allerdings denkt man da immer eher an die Käufer, den Ladeninhabern hingegen werden oft vorwiegend rationale Gründe unterstellt. Bei Markus Kastenhuber ist das anders: Ihm nimmt man schnell ab, dass er jedes Mal, wenn einem Kunden etwas gefällt, auch selbst ein bisschen glücklicher wird. Der auf Sylt aufgewachsene gelernte Kaufmann ist denn auch voller Begeisterung, als er in seinem Laden „Kegelmann" in Kampen von seiner besonderen Leidenschaft erzählt: „Ich liebe es, wenn jemand etwas Schönes findet. Die meisten Kundinnen in diesem Laden kaufen ja wirklich aus Spaß ein. Sie genießen es, in diesem wunderschön gestalteten Geschäft zu sein, sie brauchen gar nicht unbedingt ein neues Paar Schuhe oder eine Handtasche". Oder eben doch: Denn manche Wünsche wollen eben einfach erfüllt werden, und Seltenes ist immer besonders begehrt. Und viele Modelle, die Kastenhuber in seinen Läden stehen hat, sind tatsächlich nicht an jeder Ecke zu haben. So produziert zum Beispiel die Firma Unnützer in Venedig einige ihrer handgemachten Schuhmodelle speziell nach den Wünschen Kastenhubers. Die gute Zusammenarbeit mit dem Schuhdesigner Fritz Unnützer führte sogar zur Übernahme seiner Hamburger Filiale durch Markus Kastenhuber. Den beliebten Laden für Damenschuhe und Taschen in Kampen hingegen hatte Kastenhuber bereits 2006 von der Vorbesitzerin Frau Kegelmann übernommen, samt des gut eingeführten Namens und der langjähr-

MR K'S TREASURE BOXES

Many people will accept that a shopping experience can bring happiness. However, one nearly always thinks of the buyers, whereas shopkeepers are often mainly assumed to act for rational reasons. For Markus Kastenhuber it is different, and one soon accepts he is more contented each time a customer finds something pleasing. This qualified merchant who grew up on Sylt is full of enthusiasm in his shop "Kegelmann" in Kampen when he talks of his special passion: "I just love it if someone finds something beautiful. Most customers in this shop really do shop for fun. They enjoy being in this beautifully styled shop, they don't necessarily need a new pair of shoes or a handbag". Or perhaps they do, because some desires simply require fullfilling, and rare items are always in particular demand. Moreover, many designs that Kastenhuber has on display in his shop are indeed not to be found on every corner. Thus for instance the Unützer company produces in Venice some of its handmade shoe designs at special request from Kastenhuber. Good collaboration with shoe designer Fritz Unützer even led to the takeover of his Hamburg branch by Markus Kastenhuber. The popular store for ladies' shoes and bags in Kampen however, had already been taken over by Kastenhuber from the previous owner Mrs Kegelmann in 2006, along with the well-established name and the long-time, well-loved employee Gabriele Martinez. Indeed, tradition plays an important rôle when shopping on Sylt.Apart from the stores in Kampen and Hamburg, Kastenhuber also runs – partly with his brother – a store of the Gant brand in Kitzbühel as well

gen beliebten Mitarbeiterin Gabriele Martinez. Denn auch Tradition spielt eine große Rolle beim Shoppen auf Sylt. Außer den Geschäften in Kampen und Hamburg führt Kastenhuber - zum Teil gemeinsam mit seinem Bruder - auch noch einen Store der Marke Gant in Kitzbühel sowie fünf weitere Läden auf Sylt. Neben dem in Pastell-Rosé eingerichteten Shop „I Love my Shoes" am Tipkenhoog 3 in Keitum gibt es in Westerland zwei weitere Gant-Stores in der Strandstraße, das Geschäft „Kastenhuber Sylt" in der Friedrichstraße 39 und schließlich - seit 2016 ganz neu in der Shop-Familie - den Kleinen Kaschmirladen, ebenfalls in der Friedrichstraße. Jedes der vergleichsweise kleinen Geschäfte hat ein individuelles Flair, und überall versucht der Chef regelmäßig selbst vor Ort zu sein, „als Aushilfe, um den Mitarbeitern den Rücken freizuhalten", sagt er lächelnd. Markus Kastenhuber liebt jeden einzelnen seiner mit viel Geschmack und Bedacht, fast wie kleine Schatzkästchen eingerichteten CHARMING STORES: „Schöne Dinge zu verkaufen, ist meine große Leidenschaft", gesteht Markus Kastenhuber, und erzählt weiter: „Wenn ich abends mal allein vor meinen Läden stehe und mir die stimmungsvollen Lichter, die edlen Dekos und die toll arrangierten Blumen ansehe, dann geht mir immer noch das Herz auf. Das macht mich wirklich glücklich." Und genau dieses schöne Gefühl ist wohl auch das Geheimnis seines Erfolges: Denn die Kunden lieben Kastenhubers Läden ebenso, wo immer sie auch sind.

as five further stores on Sylt. Along with the "I Love my Shoes" shop furnished in pastel-pink at Tipkenhoog 3 in Keitum there are two further Gant stores in Westerland on Strandstraße, the "Kastenhuber Sylt" store at Friedrichstraße 39 and finally - since 2016 brand new in the shop-family - the little cashmere shop, also in Friedrichstraße. Each of these comparatively small businesses has an individual flair, and the manager himself seeks to regularly visit all of the shops, "as an assistant, to help the staff and back them up", he says, smiling. Markus Kastenhuber loves every one of his CHARMING STORES, each furnished, tastefully and thoughtfully almost like little treasure boxes: "Selling beautiful things is my big passion", Markus Kastenhuber admits, and further relates: "When I stand alone in front of my shops in the evening and look at the sublime lighting, the gentle decor and the gorgeously arranged flowers, then it always cheers my heart, and this really makes me happy."
And exactly this wonderful feeling is probably the secret of his success: Because the customers love Kastenhuber's shops just as much, wherever they are.

KEGELMANN
Markus Kastenhuber GmbH
Kurhausstraße 2
25999 Kampen
Telefon 046 51 / 429 04
www.kastenhuber-sylt.de

Wo will ich wohnen im Paradies?

Im Braderuper Weg 2 in Kampen betreibt Tom Kirst seinen Immobilienshop als Lizenzpartner von Dahler & Company. Die Atmosphäre ist angenehm und entspannt, genau wie Kirst selbst. Nach vielen Jahren in leitender Position bei den großen Immobilienfirmen freut er sich, seit 2007 wieder als selbstständiger Immobilienvermittler auf Sylt zu arbeiten. „Ich verbringe viel lieber Zeit mit meinen Kunden", sagt er lächelnd. Und der Erfolg gibt ihm recht, denn inzwischen gehört Kirst zu den drei größten Maklern in Kampen. Er findet es wichtig, in Kontakt mit den Bewohnern zu stehen und alle Entwicklungen ganzjährig hautnah mitzuerleben. Denn jeder regionale Markt hat seine Besonderheiten. Neben den vielen außergewöhnlichen und schönen Immobilien schätzt Kirst den Umgang mit seiner anspruchsvollen Klientel. „Ich habe hier, meist in sehr lockerer Atmosphäre, wirklich interessante Leute kennengelernt", erinnert sich Kirst, „sowohl unter den Käufern als auch unter den Verkäufern." Eine Immobilie in guter Lage ist heute mehr denn je eine optimale Geldanlage, da das Angebot knapp und die Nachfrage stets hoch ist. Tom Kirst kennt inzwischen fast alles und jeden auf dem Sylter Immobilienmarkt und findet meist eine gute Lösung: „So mancher hat sein Traumhaus auch schon an Orten gefunden, von denen er vorher noch gar nichts wusste", verrät er.

WHERE IN PARADISE DO I WISH TO LIVE?

At Braderuper Weg 2, in Kampen, Tom Kirst runs his real estate shop as a licensed partner to Dahler & Company. The atmosphere is pleasant and relaxed, just like Kirst himself. Following many years in a leading position at large real estate companies, he is happy to be once again working self-employed as a real estate agent on Sylt since 2007. "I much prefer to spend time with my clients", he says, smiling. And the success has proved him right, because meanwhile Kirst has become one of the three largest brokers in Kampen. He finds it important to remain in contact with the residents and to experience all developments first-hand all year round. This is because every regional market has its particularities. Along with the many exceptional and beautiful real estate properties, Kirst appreciates his dealings with his demanding clientele. "I have got to know truly interesting people here, mostly in a very informal atmosphere", recalls Kirst, "among the buyers as well as among the sellers". A well situated property is today more than ever an optimum investment, because supply is low and demand is always high. Tom Kirst meanwhile knows almost everything and everyone involved in Sylt's real estate market, and usually finds a good solution: "Some have even found their dream house at locations that they didn't even know about beforehand", he reveals.

TOM KIRST IMMOBILIEN GMBH & CO. KG
Dahler & Company Sylt
Braderuper Weg 2
25999 Kampen
Telefon 046 51 / 83 60 50
sylt@dahlercompany.de
www.dahlercompany.com/de/unternehmen/sylt/team-shop

Unwiderstehlich für Millionen Besucher: kilometerlanger weißer Strand an wilden Nordseewellen, gesäumt von sanften Dünen.
Simply irresistible for millions of visitors: Miles of white sand beaches with wild North Sea waves, bordered by softly undulating dunes.

Tradition und Wohnkomfort

Den Hauch der guten alten Zeit von Sylt kann man besonders in Wenningstedt hier und da noch spüren. Viele Pensionen und Gästehäuser erscheinen seit Jahrzehnten fast unverändert, und manch heutiger Sylt-Urlauber fühlt sich angenehm an seine Kindheit erinnert, als er hier sonnige Strandtage verlebte. Aber bei aller Romantik: Der Wohnkomfort sollte nicht in den Sechzigerjahren stecken geblieben sein. Niemand weiß das besser als Kirsten Kruse-Petersen vom Hotel Wiesbaden in Wenningstedt, das seit über 50 Jahren begeisterte Gäste hat. Die Sylterin führt das Hotel garni Wiesbaden, das ihre Mutter Waltraud Kruse, eine gebürtige Wiesbadenerin, nach ihrer Geburtsstadt benannt hat. Es sei wichtig, den gewachsenen Charme eines Hauses zu erhalten und nur behutsam Dinge zu verändern, betont Frau Kruse-Petersen, aber was Ausstattung, Technik und Service angehe, müsse man stets auf der Höhe der Zeit bleiben. Diese Gratwanderung klappt sehr gut, hier am Hochkamp: Viele Stammgäste, häufig aus der Generation 50 plus, buchen das strandnahe und ruhige Hotel. Besonderes äußeres Kennzeichen: Ein auffällig schöner Garten mit Strandkörben. Dazu bieten 15 stilvoll-individuelle Zimmer und 2 Ferienwohnungen allen Komfort, und die Mitarbeiter sorgen dafür, dass sich der Gast entspannt. Auch Unterhaltung und Gastronomie findet sich in Gehweite. Weiteren 50 Jahren steht ebenfalls nichts im Wege, denn die dritte Generation der Familie Kruse-Petersen arbeitet bereits im Hause mit.

TRADITION AND MODERNITY BRILLIANTLY COMBINED

Particularly in Wenningstedt one can still sense, here and there, a hint of Sylt's good old times. Many boarding houses and guest-houses appear hardly changed at all for decades, and some of today's holiday makers from Sylt are pleasantly reminded of their childhood when they spent sunny days on the beach. Although, romanticism aside: Home comforts should not remain stranded in the 60s. No-one is more aware of this than Kirsten Kruse-Petersen at the Hotel Wiesbaden in Wenningstedt, which has been receiving enthusiastic guests for over fifty years. This proprietress from Sylt runs the breakfast-only Hotel Wiesbaden, which her mother, Waltraud Kruse, named after the town of her birth in Hesse. It appears to be important to retain the accumulated charm of a property and to only carefully alter some aspects of it, Frau Kruse-Petersen emphasises, but where facilities, technical aspects and service is concerned, one must continually be in step with the times. This balancing act works very well here on Hochkamp: Many regular guests, often in their 50s and over, like to book this quiet hotel situated close to the beach. A special outdoor characteristic is the conspicuously beautiful garden with wicker beach chairs. In addition, every conceivable comfort is offered by the 15 stylish, individual rooms and 2 holiday apartments, and the staff ensure that the guests are able to relax. Entertainment and gastronomy is also to be found within walking distance. Nothing stands in the way of a further fifty years for the hotel, because the third generation of the Kruse-Petersen family already works on the premises.

HOTEL WIESBADEN
Kirsten Kruse-Petersen
Hochkamp 8
25996 Wenningstedt
Telefon 046 51 / 984 40
info@hotel-wiesbaden-sylt.de
www.hotel-wiesbaden-sylt.de

Mit dem Kutter über den Asphalt

Alles, was Vierbeiner und ihre Besitzer brauchen, findet man in Wenningstedt in der Promenadenmischung: Das kleine Geschäft von Stefanie Hausen bietet ein großes, sehr hochwertiges und oft auch überraschendes Angebot: so wie seit 2016 der „Hundekutter“ zum Mieten, ein Elektrolastenfahrrad mit einer speziellen offenen Hundekabine, was stressfreies Radeln für Hund und Mensch ermöglicht. Besonderen Wert wird in der Promenadenmischung auch auf die Nachhaltigkeit der Waren gelegt, insbesondere bei Produkten tierischen Ursprungs. „Wenn ich Tiere liebe, dann kann ich doch nicht wollen, dass für meinen Hund andere Tiere unnötig leiden müssen“, erläutert Stefanie Hausen ihr Konzept. Neben dem guten Angebot wissen Stefanie Hausens Kunden außerdem zu schätzen, dass die studierte Tierpsychologin auch als Hundetrainerin ausgebildet ist. Wenn der Hund zum Beispiel eine bestimmte Nahrung nicht mehr verträgt, kann Hausen meistens gut beurteilen, ob nur der Tierarzt oder schon eine einfache Nahrungsumstellung helfen kann. Auch bei Verhaltensauffälligkeiten der Tiere weiß Hausen eigentlich immer Rat, und sollten da die kostenlosen Tipps im Laden einmal nicht mehr ausreichen, kann bei ihr ein professionelles Einzel- und Gruppentraining gebucht werden.

„Oft hilft den Leuten schon ein einfacher Hinweis weiter“, sagt Stefanie Hausen und fügt hinzu: „Ich freue mich, wenn ich das Zusammenleben von Hund und Mensch verbessern kann.“ – und das wissen ihre Kunden zu schätzen, auch die vierbeinigen.

STEERING THE SLOOP OVER THE ASPHALT

Everything which four-legged friends and their owners require, can be found in Wenningstedt in the Promenadenmischung shop: This small business managed by Stefanie Hausen has a large, very high quality, and often quite surprising range of goods on offer: such as for example since 2016 the Hundekutter (the dog sloop) for hire, an electro cargo-bicycle with a special, open cabin for dogs, which enables stress-free cycling for dog and owner.

In Promenadenmischung, special consideration is given to the sustainability of all articles, especially to items with an animal-product source. “If I love animals, then I certainly do not want other animals to unnecessarily have to suffer for the benefit of my own dog”, explains Stefanie Hausen about her concept.

Along with the good range of articles on offer in her shop, customers also appreciate that Stefanie Hausen is a qualified dog trainer who studied animal psychology. When for example a dog can no longer tolerate a certain food, Hausen can usually determine whether a visit to the vet is necessary or whether simply a change of diet would suffice. Dog behavioural problems are also concerns for which Hausen always has some advice, and if perhaps on one occasion gratis tips from her in her shop prove to be insufficient, professional, individual or group training with her can be booked. “Very often a simple piece of advice will help the customers further”, says Stefanie Hausen and adds: “I am always very pleased to be able to improve the coexistence between dog and owner.” – and her customers appreciate this very much, their four-legged friends as well.

PROMENADENMISCHUNG
Stefanie Hausen
Hauptstraße 8–10
25996 Wennigstedt
Telefon 046 51 / 967 66 70
info@promenadenmischung-sylt.de
www.promenadenmischung-sylt.de

Après-Beach und Topgenuss

Die Seestraße in Wenningstedt wäre eine eher unauffällige Wohngegend, gäbe es hier nicht diese kleine gemütliche Holzhütte. Wenige Meter vom Strandzugang entfernt, steht Ivo & Co. Bistro und Weine, auf Sylt berühmt für edle Burger, selbst gemachte Pommes frites und tolle Weine. Einst gab es hier den Pottkieker, eine beliebte Imbissbude. Gründer und Sommelier Ivo Köster machte daraus 2012 einen Imbiss deluxe mit Fast Food auf Feinschmeckerniveau. Dazu: Eine erlesene Weinkarte. Nico Torbahn und sein Frau Juliane Gehrt übernahmen das erfolgreiche Lokal samt Konzept und Namen 2014. Nachhaltige Produkte aus der Region in absoluter Topqualität sind dabei die Grundlage ihres kulinarischen Angebots. Die Karte des Bistros ist absichtlich klein gehalten, bietet aber garantiert Gaumenfreuden für jeden Geschmack und auch für jedes Alter. Juliane und Nico haben hier ihren Traum verwirklicht. In dem kleinen Laden, der auch Tische im Außenbereich anbietet, herrscht stets eine entspannte familiäre Stimmung, selbst wenn es einmal eng wird und sich Warteschlangen bilden. Reservierungen gibt es bewusst nicht und das Essen nur per Bedienung an den Tischen. Alternativ kann man seine Bestellung aber auch „zum Mitnehmen" bekommen und dann am nahen Strand genießen. Aber die Zeit wird den Gästen des Bistros nur selten lang, denn Nico und sein Team verstehen es, ihre Kundschaft auch zu Stoßzeiten mit viel guter Laune und einem kühlen Getränk vorab bei der Stange zu halten.

APRÈS BEACH AND TOP ENJOYMENT

Seestraße in Wenningstedt would otherwise be a quite inconspicuous residential area, if it was not for this cosy little wooden hut. Only a few metres from the beach entrance, there stands Ivo & Co. Bistro und Weine, famous on Sylt for its upscale burgers, self-made French fries and fine wines. Once, the 'Pottkieker' existed here, a much loved snack bar. In 2012, founder and sommelier Ivo Köster turned it into a snack stall deluxe, with fast food on a gourmet niveau. In addition: an exquisite wine list. Nico Torbahn and his wife Juliane Gehrt took over the successful premises including its concept and name in 2014. Sustainable regional produce in absolute top quality are included as the basis of their culinary selection. The menu of the bistro has intentionally been kept small, but it offers guaranteed fine delicacies for every taste and also for every age group. Here, Juliane and Nico have realised their dream. On these small premises, which also offer outdoor tables, there always exists a relaxed familial environment, even when it becomes rather full and queues begin to form. There are certainly no reservations accepted here and the food is only through service at the tables. Alternatively, one can however have one's order 'to go' and then enjoy it on the nearby beach. Although, time seldom appears to be very long here for the bistro's guests, since Nico and his team know how to keep their customers on board even during busy times, and in a good mood with a cool drink in advance.

IVO & CO. BISTRO UND WEINE
Inhaber: Nico Torbahn
Seestrasse 29
25996 Wenningstedt
Telefon: 046 51/995 67 69
info@ivoundco-bistro.de
www.ivoundco-bistro.de

DÖNNHOFF
Riesling
trocken
2014
NAHE
IVO & CO.
Bistro & Weine
Tel.: 04651 - 9956769
Seestr. 29, 25996 Wenningstedt
www.ivoundco-bistro.de
Salate
Frischer Caesarsalat
mit
-marinierter Hühnchenbrust
-gebratenen Scampi
Bunter Salat
- Hühnchenstreifen
- Scampi
8,50
12,00
14,50
9,00
11,50
14,00
Suppen
6,90

Folgen Sie dem Weg: Das Grüne Kliff in Keitum ist wunderschön. Lassen Sie sich etwas Zeit und genießen Sie den Ausblick.
Follow the track: The Green Cliff in Keitum is beautiful. Take your time and enjoy the view.

Zwischen Marsch und Kliff

Obwohl es natürlich überall auf der Insel gute Unterkünfte gibt, liegen die größten Bettenkapazitäten in der Nähe der westlichen Badestrände. Und so kann es durchaus vorkommen, dass manch einem Urlauber andere Seiten der Insel unbekannt bleiben. Dies trifft vor allem auf Teile der sogenannten Nösse-Halbinsel zu (Nösse kommt aus dem Friesischen und bedeutet so viel wie Landzunge). Diese beginnt hinter Tinnum und erstreckt sich mit den Ortschaften Keitum, Archsum und Morsum bis zum östlichen Ende der Insel am Hindenburgdamm. Fast allen Sylt-Besuchern ein Begriff ist wohl noch Keitum: In dem malerischen ehemaligen Hauptort der Insel ließen sich früher viele Kapitäne, Fischer und Walfänger nieder. Der ehemals bedeutende Hafen ist längst verschwunden, aber zwischen Grünem Kliff und Bahnlinie finden sich immer noch unzählige hübsche und teilweise sehr alte Häuser. Der Ort ist verkehrsberuhigt und so lässt sich beim gemächlichen Rundgang durch die manchmal etwas labyrinthisch anmutenden kleinen Wege und Straßen immer wieder etwas Neues entdecken: Es gibt eine erstaunliche Vielfalt an Restaurants und Geschäften, Kulturinteressierte kommen in den sehenswerten Heimatmuseen und schönen Galerien auf ihre Kosten und am westlichen Ortsrand kann die Kirche Sankt Severin besichtigt werden. Auf ihrem Friedhof haben

BETWEEN MARSH AND CLIFF

Although there is meanwhile plenty of accommodation on the whole of the island, the majority of holiday makers still tend to stay near the island's western bathing beaches. It therefore sometimes occurs that the island's other side remains unknown to many. This is above all true for part of the so-called Nösse peninsular (Nösse is from Frisian and essentially means spit of land). It begins just beyond Tinnum and, including the villages of Keitum, Archsum and Morsum, stretches to the eastern end of the island at Hindenburg Dam. One name probably known to almost all Sylt visitors is Keitum: In this, the island's picturesque former main town, many captains, fishermen and whalers took up residence here in the past. The previously important harbour disappeared long ago, but between grassy cliffs and the railway line there are still numerous pretty and to some extent very old houses to be found. The village is traffic-calmed, so a leisurely walkabout through the sometimes seemingly labyrinthine small alleyways and streets often leads to a few new discoveries: There is an astounding diversity of restaurants and shops, culture enthusiasts will certainly get their money's worth in the impressive local museums and handsome galleries, and on the village's western edge the church of St Severin may be visited. A whole array of famous Sylt natives and Sylt residents found their last resting place in the village cemetery. On the east-

Auch das ist Sylt: einfaches norddeutsches Landleben, manchmal mit Meeresblick für Kuh und Mensch.
This is Sylt as well: Simple North German country living, sometimes with a sea view for cows and people.

eine ganze Reihe berühmter Sylter und Wahlsylter ihre letzte Ruhe gefunden. Am östlichen Rand Keitums liegen außerdem die vorgeschichtlichen Megalithgräber Tipkenhoog und Harhoog. Aber auch außerhalb Keitums gibt es viel Schönes zu entdecken: Auf der Südhälfte der Halbinsel haben die ungewöhnlich ruhigen Wege in der ländlichen Marsch oder beim Nösse-Deich ihren besonderen Reiz. Inmitten der Landzunge liegt kurz hinter dem Übergang zur nördlichen Geesthälfte die kleinste Ortschaft Sylts: das angenehm unspektakuläre Archsum. Wunderbare Möglichkeiten zum Spazierengehen finden sich an der nördlichen Wattkante zwischen dem Grünen Kliff bei Keitum und dem Morsum-Kliff. Das Sylter Wattenmeer und die Küstenlandschaft mit ihrer faszinierenden Pflanzen- und Tierwelt lassen sich kaum irgendwo auf der Insel besser genießen als hier. Und mit dem bis zu 21 Meter hohen und 1,8 Kilometer langen Morsum-Kliff besitzt Sylt eines der wichtigsten geologischen Denkmäler Deutschlands – in seinen Gesteinsschichten werden immer wieder bedeutende Fossilien entdeckt. Das nahe Morsum mit seinen etwas verstreut liegenden, ländlich geprägten Ortsteilen bietet in der Nähe des Bahnhofs gute Möglichkeiten zum Einkehren und Einkaufen. Mit der Bahn kann der Ausflügler von Morsum aus dann in wenigen Minuten wieder in Westerland sein.

ern edge of Keitum there are in addition the prehistoric megalithic tombs of Tipkenhoog and Harhoog. However, beyond Keitum there are many other beatiful things to see in Sylt's east: Certainly the unusually peaceful trails in the marsh and on the Nösse dike, and even the Rantum basin all have their own particular attraction. In the midst of the land spit shortly after the transition to the northern geest portion lies Sylt's smallest locale: the pleasantly unspectacular Archsum. Wonderful opportunities for walks can be found on the northern edge of the mudflats between the green cliff near Keitum and Morsum Cliff. The Wadden Sea at Sylt and its coastal landscape with fascinating flora and fauna can hardly better be enjoyed anywhere else on the island. And with Morsum Cliff, Sylt has one of the most important geological monuments in Germany – significant fossil finds are always turning up here in the diversely coloured rock strata. Nearby Morsum, with its somewhat scattered, rurally characterised outer districts, offers good opportunities for shopping or stopping off for a bite to eat near to the railway station. By rail from Morsum, excursionists can again reach Westerland in only a few minutes.

Ein Spaziergang am Watt ist ein unvergessliches Naturerlebnis. Das Morsum-Kliff ein lohnendes Ziel.
A walk at Wadden Sea is an unforgettable, natural experience. Morsum Cliff is a worthwhile destination.

Etwas skeptisch scheint dieser Krabbe die Touristen zu beäugen. Die meisten Besucher respektieren aber den Naturschutz.
This crab seems to view the tourists with a little scepticism. Most visitors however, respect nature conservancy.

Raffelhüschen

Der Herr der Brötchen

Zu früher Morgenstunde geht es auf Sylt, mal abgesehen von ein paar Lieferanten oder Berufspendlern, selbst in der Hochsaison noch relativ ruhig zu. Mit einer großen Ausnahme: Filialen der Bäckerei Raffelhüschen. Hier haben sich meistens bereits lange, oft etwas ungeduldige Schlangen von Brötchenholern gebildet. Motto: Wer zuerst kommt, der knuspert auch zuerst in der Ferienwohnung. Die gute Nachfrage an den zwölf Standorten ist natürlich ein Kompliment. Aber Juniorchef Thomas Raffelhüschen schmunzelt auch ein wenig über dieses morgendliche Phänomen: Eigentlich brauche sich doch keiner zu beeilen, es gebe ausreichend Brötchen für alle. Vater Broder und Sohn Thomas Raffelhüschen, welcher nun in der vierten Bäckergeneration Sylt mit Brot, Brötchen, Kuchen und anderen Backwaren versorgt, haben ihre Erfahrungswerte. Ist die Insel voller Urlauber und das Wetter am nächsten Tag gut, stellt man sich in der Tinnumer Backstube darauf ein. Bis zu 30 000 Brötchen können es an so einem Tag dann schon mal werden. Auch den Geschmack seiner Kunden kennt Raffelhüschen natürlich gut: Der absolute Brötchen-Renner ist der Dünenknust, ebenso hat der Sylter Knacker, fast ein kleines Roggenbrot, seine Fans. Und wenn es doch mal etwas nicht gibt, hat das meist einen guten Grund: Bei gutem Wetter werden zum Beispiel weniger Sahnetorten und mehr „Bürgermeister" gebacken. Der Marzipanplunder kann nämlich besser mit der Hitze umgehen – eben ein echter Sylter Strandprofi.

LORD OF THE BREAD ROLLS

Apart from a few deliveries or some commuters during the early morning hours on Sylt, things remain relatively calm, even in the high season. With one big exception: the branches of the Raffelhüschen bakery. Here there are often quite impatient queues of customers waiting for fresh rolls, which have been forming, some for quite a while. The slogan here is: Whoever arrives on time will also be the first to crunch fresh rolls in their holiday apartment. The high demand at these twelve locations is of course a compliment in itself. However, junior director Thomas Raffelhüschen grins a little about this morning phenomenon: No-one really needs to hurry, there are sufficient fresh products for everyone. Father Broder and his son Thomas Raffelhüschen, now in their fourth baker generation, who have been supplying Sylt with bread, rolls, cakes and other bakery goods, have plenty of experience to draw on. If the island if full with holiday makers and the weather on the following day is going to be fine, then one adjusts one's calculations in the Tinnumer bakery accordingly. This could mean up to 30,000 rolls being required on such a day. Raffelhüschen also knows the taste of his customers well: The absolute top attraction is the Dünenknust, the 'dune crust' and in the same way the Sylter Knacker, almost a small rye loaf that also has its fans. And when indeed there is a lack of a product there is usually a good reason for it: During fine weather for instance fewer gâteaux will be baked and more 'Bürgermeister'. This marzipan pastry can better withstand the heat of a warm day – that is, a true Sylt beach pro.

BÄCKEREI RAFFELHÜSCHEN GMBH & CO. KG
Geschäftsführer:
Broder Raffelhüschen
Thomas Raffelhüschen
Zum Fliegerhorst 20
25980 Sylt / OT Tinnum
Telefon 046 51 / 223 78
www.raffelhueschen-sylt.de

Fokussieren, loslassen, treffen

Die antike nordische Göttin Youksakka verkörpert Besinnung, Ernährung, Schutz, Gesundheit und Wohlstand, und als Hüterin der Bogenschießkunst ist sie die Namensgeberin der Youksakka Bow & Funcompany. Hier auf ihrem Schießplatz beim Tinnumer Sportzentrum merkt man schnell, dass es um viel mehr geht als um Treffer in der Zielscheibe. Peter Berhorst und sein Team unterrichten Schüler aller Altersgruppen im Bogenbau und vor allem in der Kunst des intuitiven Bogenschießens. „Ruhe, Konzentration und geschärfte Wahrnehmung sind gleichzeitig Weg und Ziel der Übungen“, erklärt Peter Berhorst, „am Bogen wird der Aufbau der richtigen Körperspannung trainiert, die sich dann mit dem Schuss wieder löst.“ So entsteht nach und nach ein Gefühl für Pfeil und Bogen, aber auch die eigene Intuition und das Körpergefühl werden positiv weiterentwickelt. „Im Kopf der Schüler passiert hier ganz viel“, ergänzt Berhorst, „egal, ob Kind oder Erwachsener, der Zuwachs an Selbstvertrauen ist jedes Mal enorm.“ Kein Wunder, dass diese Art des Schießens inzwischen auch als Managertraining gefragt ist. Auch die Youksakka-Bogenbaukurse sind sehr beliebt: Nach historischen Plänen stellen die Kursteilnehmer unter fachkundiger Anleitung eigenen Bögen aus verschiedenen Hölzern her. Nebenbei werden gesellschaftliche und historische Zusammenhänge rund um das Thema Bogenschießen vermittelt. Und das Konzept kommt an: „Die meisten Schüler kommen wieder“, freut sich Peter Berhorst, „und es werden immer mehr.“

TAKE AIM, LOOSE, STRIKE

The ancient Nordic goddess Youksakka embodied consciousness, nourishment, protection, health and wealth, and as the guardian of archery she is the eponym of the Youksakka Bow & Funcompany. Here at its archery range at the Tinnum sports centre one soon realises that there is much more going on than just hitting the target circle. Peter Berhorst and his team teach their students of all age groups about bowyer craftsmanship and above all about the art of intuitive shooting with bow and arrows. “Composure, concentration and sharpened perception are at the same time the path and goal of the exercises”, explains Peter Berhorst, “training with the bow develops the correct body tension, which then recedes when the arrow is loosed.” Thus emerges, bit by bit, a feeling for the arrow and the bow, but also one’s own intuition and body awareness are positively further developed. “In the student’s mind there is a lot going on here”, Berhorst adds, “Every time, no matter whether child or adult, the growth of self-confidence is tremendous”. No wonder then, that meanwhile this type of shooting is also in high demand in manager training. The Youksakka bowyer courses are also very popular: In accordance with historical plans, the course participants produce their own bows from various types of wood under expert guidance. In addition, socio-historical relationships are taught about all aspects of shooting with bow and arrows. And the concept is catching on: “The majority of our students return”, Peter Berhorst is pleased to announce, “and more and more are coming here.”

YOUKSAKKA BOW & FUNCOMPANY
Keitumer Landstraße, am Sportzentrum Sylt-Ost
25980 Sylt / OT Tinnum
Telefon 01 77 / 80 27 30 9
info@youksakka.de
www.youksakka.de

17
76
No 4

Vom Fremdenzimmer zum Topappartement

In dem schönen alten Haus am Gurtstig 37 in Keitum hat die Appartementvermietung Maike Ossenbrüggen ihr Büro, und die Besucher können hier einem Stück Inselgeschichte nachspüren: Denn hier lebte Maike Ossenbrüggen (1939–2014), ein echtes Sylter Urgestein, Vorsitzende des Sylter Heimatvereins Söl'ring Foriining und beliebte Vermieterin unzähliger Urlaubsgäste. Jennifer Daberkow hat noch mit ihr zusammengearbeitet und führt als neue Inhaberin ganz bewusst den traditionsreichen Firmennamen weiter. Genau wie dieser früher schon für einen herzlichen Umgang und ein reelles Angebot stand, so werden die Urlauber auch heute stets authentisch und mit Herz beraten. „Das fängt schon bei der komplett neu gestalteten Website an. Auf dem neuster Stand der Technik werden unsere Feriendomizile mit aktuellen und realistischen Fotos präsentiert", erklärt Daberkow, „für meine Mitarbeiter und mich ist es auch selbstverständlich, dass wir den Gast in die Ferienwohnung begleiten und es immer Blumen sowie ein Begrüßungspräsent gibt." Der Kunde kann sich in allen Kategorien auf die Qualität der charmanten Mietobjekte verlassen: „Seit den Anfängen von Frau Ossenbrüggen hat sich nicht nur auf Sylt, sondern auch in der Agentur hinsichtlich des Gastanspruchs viel geändert", resümiert Jennifer Daberkow. Was sich aber nicht geändert hat, ist das offene Ohr für die Gäste und auch mal die Zeit für einen Schnack hier im Büro – wie damals bei Maike Ossenbrüggen.

FROM GUEST ROOM TO TOP APARTMENT

In the beautiful old house at Gurtstig 37 in Keitum the apartment rental service Maike Ossenbrüggen has its office, and visitors here can trace a piece of island history: because between 1939 and 2014 Maike Ossenbrüggen lived here. She was a genuine institution on Sylt and chairwoman of Sylt's local traditions society in Söl'ring Foriining as well as being a well-respected rental agent for countless holiday guests. Jennifer Daberkow was fortunate to have worked with her and, and also this new proprietress quite consciously continues to use the long-standing family name. Just as this name once stood for sincerity and a fair offer, so too are holiday makers today given advice that is always genuine and heartfelt. "This already begins with the completely new design of our website. Using the latest technologies, our holiday properties will be presented using current and realistic photos", explains Daberkow, "for my staff and for myself it is also natural that we shall accompany the guests into their holiday apartments and always offer fresh flowers as well as a welcoming gift". In every aspect, the customer can be assured of the quality of the charming rental properties: "Since the very beginnings of Frau Ossenbrüggen much has changed, and not only on Sylt but also in the agency, with regard to the requirements of the guests", summarizes Jennifer Daberkow. That which has not changed though, is being all ears for the guests and perhaps also finding time for the odd chat here in the office – just as it once was for Maike Ossenbrüggen.

APPARTEMENTVERMIETUNG MAIKE OSSENBRÜGGEN
Inhaberin: Jennifer Daberkow
Gurtstig 37
25980 Sylt / OT Keitum
Telefon 046 51 / 315 07
info@fewoaufsylt.de
www.fewoaufsylt.de

Brot und Bier für die Insel

Alexandro Pape ist nicht nur den Feinschmeckern des Landes ein Begriff. Eines seiner zahlreichen kulinarischen Projekte nach dem Ausstieg aus der Zwei-Sterne-Küche heißt Brot & Bier. Mit diesem Bistro in Keitum erfreuen Pape und sein Team seit Mai 2016 ihre zahlreichen Gäste von Sylt und anderswo. Neben einem großen hellen Gastraum gibt es hier auch einen kleinen Shop, in dem man ausgewählte Produkte und natürlich Brot und Bier zum Mitnehmen findet. Das kulinarische Konzept ist einfach und lecker: „Wir wollen das gute alte Ritual des Abendbrotes wieder in den Fokus rücken", erläutert Pape, „von der Mettstulle bis zur Lachsstulle wird das belegte Brot hier ganz neu interpretiert – mit Ideen aus der anspruchsvollen Küche." Und natürlich ist alles von meisterlicher Qualität, was hier ab 12 Uhr auf den Tisch kommt. Die „Stullenmacher" Alexandro Pape, Sven Pietschmann und Tim Grauel erschaffen auf Basis der täglich frisch und exklusiv gebackenen acht Brotsorten ständig neue kleine Gerichte. Etwa ein Dutzend warmer, kalter sowie süßer und deftiger Versionen an Brot kann man im Brot & Bier bestellen. Neben anderen Fass- und Flaschenbieren wird vor allem die Eigenmarke WATT Blondes empfohlen. Dieses leichte, obergärige Bier wird erst seit 2016 in den Räumlichkeiten von Papes Sylter Genussmacherei in List gebraut. Das Wasser stammt aus dem reinen Kondensat der Salzgewinnung, was wahrscheinlich weltweit einmalig ist. Brot wie Bier werden also wieder zum Erlebnis – im Brot & Bier.

BREAD AND BEER FOR THE ISLE

Alexandro Pape is not only a notable name for epicureans around the country. One of his many culinary projects following his departure from two-star cuisine is called 'Brot & Bier'. With this bistro in Keitum, Pape and his team have been delighting their many guests from Sylt and elsewhere since May 2016. Alongside a large bright seating area there is also a small shop in which selected products, including bread and beer of course, can be purchased to take home. The culinary concept is simple and tasty: "We aim to bring the good old ritual of supper, a light evening meal, back into focus", explains Pape, "from the Mett-stulle (pork-spread bread slice) to the Lachs-stulle (bread slice topped with salmon), open sandwiches are being completely reinterpreted here – with ideas from discerning cuisine." Of course everything which is served at the tables here from 12:00 noon is of outstanding quality. On the basis of the daily fresh, and exclusively baked, eight types of bread, the 'stulle-makers' Alexandro Pape, Sven Pietschmann and Tim Grauel are continually creating new small meals. Around a dozen different warm or cold, sweet or savoury bread versions can be ordered in Brot & Bier. As well as various draught and bottled beers, their own brand WATT Blondes is above all recommended. Brewing this light, top-fermented beer began only in 2016 on the premises of Pape's Sylter Genussmacherei in List. The required water originates from the pure condensate arising from the salt extraction there, which is probably also quite unique worldwide. Bread as well as beer once again become an experience – at Brot & Bier.

BROT & BIER
Gastronomischer Gastgeber:
Alexandro Pape
Gurtstig 1
25980 Sylt / OT Keitum
Telefon: 046 51 / 936 37 43
reservierung@brot-und-bier.de
www.brot-und-bier.de

GEBRAUT
IN DER
Sylter
GENUSS
MACHEREI
WATT
BLONDES
DAS BIER AUS DER NORDSEE

Erlesene Noblesse

Schon aus der Ferne verspricht das Weiß und das Grau des Kontorhauses in den Keitumer Wiesen ein fein abgestimmtes Zusammenspiel zwischen außen und innen.

In jedem einzelnen Raum des Suitenhotels zeigt sich das durchdachte und stilsichere Konzept des Architektenehepaares Franziska und Wolfgang Zaeske: ein Versprechen, das räumliche Großzügigkeit, Freiheit für die Sinne und eine noble Ästhetik verspricht. Jede der acht Suiten verfügt über einen Balkon oder eine Terrasse. Breite, raumhohe Fenster lassen das Innere und das Äußere ineinanderfließen. Der Blick aus den Suiten geht weit über die Keitumer Wiesen, zum Deich oder zur Keitumer Kirche Sankt Severin. Die schlichte Schönheit zeitloser Möbel verleiht den Suiten eine wohlige Atmosphäre, die Nacht wird in den wunderbaren Betten zur traumhaften Erholung. Highlights wie die frei stehende Badewanne von Philippe Starck sorgen darüber hinaus für galaktische Luxusmomente: Genau richtig positioniert, kann der Hotelgast von hier aus, in wohltemperiertem Badewasser liegend, in den Sylter Nachthimmel schauen. Eine weitere Krönung der hochwertigen Ausstattung ist die drei Meter hohe Regendusche, die den Start in einen neuen Urlaubstag zu einem magischen Erlebnis werden lässt. Im Teeraum wird allmorgendlich von engagierten Mitarbeitern ein Frühstück mit heimischen Produkten auf den Tisch gezaubert. Am selben Ort zur Teestunde am Nachmittag sorgt ein Pianist für die passende musikalische Untermalung. Nicht nur Hausgäste, sondern jeder, der die ein-

SELECT NOBLESSE

Even from a distance the white and grey of the trading house in the Keitum meadows promises a delicately harmonised interplay between the outside and indoors. In every single room of the suite hotel, the thoroughly thought out and confidently stylish concept of the architectural couple Franziska and Wolfgang Zaeske manifests itself: a promise that affirms spaciousness, freedom for the senses and a noble aesthetic. Each of the eight suites has a balcony or a terrace. Wide, floor-to-ceiling windows allow the interiors and the outdoors to merge. The view from the suites reaches far across the Keitum meadows, to the dike or to Keitum's Church of St Severin. The plain beauty of timeless furniture imparts in the suites a languorous atmosphere, nights in the hotel's wonderful beds are dreamlike relaxation. Highlights such as the free-standing bathtub from Philippe Stark ensure furthermore galactic luxury moments: Perfectly positioned, the hotel guest lying in well-tempered bathwater, can look up into Sylt's night sky. A further high point of the high-quality furnishing is the three-metre high rainshower, creating a magical experience at the start of a new vacation day. Every morning in the tea room, dedicated staff conjure up a breakfast of local produce onto your table. At the same place at teatime in the afternoons a pianist ensures a suitable musical backdrop. Not only house guests but anyone who appreciates this uniquely relaxing aura of the tea room is very welcome. Throughout the day, along with tea and pastries, other drinks and even light meals are served. The large window façade

zigartige, entspannte Aura des Teeraums zu schätzen weiß, ist herzlich willkommen. Neben Tee und Gebäck werden hier tagsüber weitere Getränke und sogar kleine Speisen serviert. Die große Fensterfront und die Terrasse sind Richtung Süden auf die einmalige Marschlandschaft ausgerichtet – der ideale Ort für eine Auszeit vom Alltag. Der ursprüngliche Teil des Kontorhauses Keitum ist das Teekontor: Hier werden exzellente Tees feinster Provenienz verkauft. Außer mit Tees und dem entsprechenden Zubehör ist der Verkaufsraum angefüllt mit erlesenen Kostbarkeiten – liebevoll zusammengetragen aus aller Welt. Die Zaeskes holen sie nach Keitum, damit die Besucher eine kleine Entdeckungsreise im Teekontor starten können. Für besonders interessierte Kunden werden auch Teeseminare angeboten. Einige Male im Jahr verwandelt sich das Teekontor in eine Kleinbühne. Dann empfangen Franziska und Wolfgang Zaeske ihre Gäste mit Sekt, Tee und Gebäck zu einer Performance zur Teestunde, immer an einem Sonntag um 17 Uhr. Die intime Atmosphäre sowie die hohe Qualität der auftretenden Künstler sind eine feste und beliebte Instanz im Sylter Kulturleben geworden.

So ist es dem Ehepaar Zaeske gelungen, in den letzten zehn Jahren seine Philosophie und seinen Lebensstil im Kontorhaus Keitum zu verwirklichen. Wer Ästhetik und entspannende Sinnlichkeit schätzt, hebt am Siidik in Keitum einen Schatz.

and the terrace face south towards the unique marsh landscape – the ideal place for time-out from everyday life. The oldest part of Kontorhaus Keitum is the Teekontor (tea store): excellent teas of the finest provenance are sold here. Apart from being well stocked with teas and their respective accessories the sales room is filled with select precious items – lovingly assembled from all around the world. The Zaeskes bring these to Keitum so that visitors can begin a small voyage of discovery in the tea store. For those customers who are especially interested, tea seminars are also on offer. For a few times each year, the Teekontor t-ansforms into a small stage. Franziska and Wolfgang Zaeske then greet their guests with sparkling wine, tea and pastries for a performance at teatime, always on a Sunday at 17:00. The intimate setting as well as the high quality of the performers appearing on stage have become a regular and popular instance in Sylt's cultural life. And so in the last ten years the Zaeskes have succeeded in realising their philosophy and lifestyle in the Kontorhaus Keitum. Those who appreciate aesthetics and relaxing sensuousness, are truly yielding a hoard, along Siidik, in Keitum.

TEEKONTOR KEITUM GMBH
Franziska und Wolfgang Zaeske
Siidik 15
25980 Sylt / OT Keitum
Telefon 046 51 / 889 11 94
tee@teekontorkeitum.de
www.teekontorkeitum.com

KONTORHAUS KEITUM

KLEINE
KÜCHENKATE
zu Gast bei Familie Sprengkamp

Essen, wie es sein soll

„Zu Gast bei Familie Sprengkamp" steht auf dem Schild der Kleinen Küchenkate in Keitum. Es könnte auch heißen: Zu Hause bei Familie Sprengkamp. Denn es gibt immer frisch zubereitetes Essen, das im Wohlfühl-Ambiente nett serviert wird. Die Sprengkamps, Gastronomen mit jahrzehntelanger Sylt-Erfahrung, konnten das schön gelegene Restaurant mit der großen Terrasse 2015 übernehmen, und man merkt, dass sie hier glücklich sind. Denn auch die Gäste kommen gern in die Küchenkate: zum Mittag, zu Kaffee und Kuchen, zum Abendessen und auch danach noch auf einen Drink – zumindest abends ist deshalb eine Reservierung empfehlenswert. Praktisch alles auf der Speisekarte stammt „vom Land und Meer" Schleswig-Holsteins oder des nahen Dänemarks, natürlich auch das Fleisch: „Ich kaufe nur bei Schlachtern meines Vertrauens, die mir genau sagen können, woher die Tiere kommen", betont Sprengkamp. Neben dem Sylter Gallowayrind empfiehlt er besonders das Schweinefleisch aus den nahen Uthlanden: „Auch da können Sie sicher sein, dass die Tiere natürlich aufwachsen und keine Hormone oder Antibiotika bekommen." Neben Fleischspezialitäten gibt es auch Fischgerichte und diverse andere Speisen. Kinder wie Erwachsene lieben außerdem das leckere Softeis in der Küchenkate, das natürlich auch „auf die Hand" verkauft wird. „Bei rechtzeitiger Vorbestellung koche ich zudem gern einmal etwas, das nicht auf der Karte steht", bietet Sprengkamp noch an und eilt dann wieder in seine Küche – die Gäste haben Hunger!

FOOD, AS IT SHOULD BE

The sign outside Kleinen Küchenkate in Keitum reads 'Zu Gast bei Familie Sprengkamp' (guest of the Sprengkamp family). It could just as well be 'at home with the Sprengkamp family'because there is always freshly prepared food nicely served in a feel-good ambience. The Sprengkamps, restaurateurs with decades of Sylt experience, were able to take over their well-situated restaurant with its large terrace in 2015, and you notice they are happy here. The guests also gladly come to Küchenkate at lunchtime, for coffee and cake, for dinner, and afterwards for a drink as well – thus at least in the evenings a reservation is recommended. Almost everything on the menu comes from Schleswig-Holstein's 'land and sea' or from nearby Denmark, and of course the meat too: "I buy only from abbatoirs I trust, who can tell me exactly where the animals come from", Sprengkamp points out. Along with Sylt's Galloway beef he especially recommends the pork from the nearby Uthlande region: "Here too you can be sure the animals are free-range and do not receive hormones or antibiotics." As well as meat specialities, there are also fish dishes and various other choices. Children and adults moreover love Küchenkate's tasty soft ice cream that is also sold to-go. "If I get an advance order in good time, I'm glad sometimes to cook something that isn't on the menu", Sprengkamp says, and then hurries off to his kitchen – the guests are hungry!

KLEINE KÜCHENKATE
Familie Sprengkamp
Hoyerstig 2
25980 Sylt / OT Keitum
Telefon 046 51 / 333 87
info@kleinekuechenkate.de
www.kleinekuechenkate.de

Ausflugsziel Bäckerei

Jürgen Ingwersen wurde dort geboren, wo heute jeden Tag viele Frühstücke serviert werden: im Café der Bäckerei & Konditorei Ingwersen in Morsum. Seit 1925 ist sie, neben Kliff und Bahnhof, wohl der bekannteste Platz des Dorfes und eine echte Institution auf der Insel Sylt. Es gehört jedoch viel Geschick dazu, so lange erfolgreich zu bleiben. „Man muss sich etwas einfallen lassen", sagt Jürgen Ingwersen, „die Konkurrenz schläft nicht, und die Leute kaufen immer mehr Backwaren im Supermarkt." An Ideen fehlt es dem Bäckermeister allerdings ebenso wenig wie an Entschlusskraft. Vor ein paar Jahren verkaufte Ingwersen seine 13 Filialen und konzentrierte sich ganz auf das Morsumer Stammhaus. Er erweiterte das Café durch einen modernen Wintergarten, stellte mehrere Köche und Servicekräfte ein und kann heute mindestens 85 Personen gleichzeitig bewirten. Dazu kommen bei schönem Wetter noch die Plätze auf der Terrasse. Die Bäckerei ist zum beliebten Ausflugsziel geworden: Absoluter Verkaufsschlager ist Ingwersens Frühstück, das in mehreren Versionen täglich von 8 bis 18 Uhr serviert wird. Eine kleine, aber sehr hochwertige Tageskarte mit warmen Gerichten ergänzt das Angebot. Zum Kaffee am Nachmittag gilt Ingwersens Rosentorte als besondere Spezialität des Hauses. Jürgen Ingwersen empfiehlt in der Saison aber dringend eine Reservierung: „Ich habe hier 80 Fahrradständer anbauen lassen, aber selbst die reichen oft nicht aus!", sagt er lächelnd.

DESTINATION BAKERY

Jürgen Ingwersen was born here, where every day many breakfasts are now served: in the café of the Bäckerei & Konditorei Ingwersen in Morsum. Since1925, it is, along with the cliffs and the railway station, perhaps one of the most well known places in the village and a real institution on the islanc of Sylt. A lot of skill is however required to remain so successful for so long. "One needs to come up with something", says Jürgen Ingwersen, "your competitors never rest, and the people buy ever more baked goods from the supermarket". However, the master baker is not lacking in ideas, nor in the least in decisiveness. A few years ago Ingwersen sold his 13 branch outlets and concentrated entirely on the Morsum main property. He expanded the café with a modern winter garden, employed more cooks and service personnel and he can now cater for at least 85 persons at the same time. In addition, there are the spaces available on the terrace during fine weather. The bakery has become a favourite excursion destination: An absolute commercial success is Ingwersen's breakfast, which is served daily in various versions from 08:00 to 18:00. A small but very high-class carte du jour containing warm meals completes the offer. With coffee during the afternoons, Ingwersen's rose gâteaux is considered to be one of the special delights of the house. During the season however, Jürgen Ingwersen strongly recommends a reservation: "I have had 80 bicycle stands constructed here, but even these are often not enough!" He says, smiling.

BÄCKEREI & KONDITOREI INGWERSEN
Jürgen Ingwersen GmbH & Co. KG
Terpstig 76
25980 Sylt / OT Morsum
Telefon: 046 51 / 82 33 42
info@ingwersen-sylt.de
www.ingwersen-sylt.de

Eine Himmelstreppe? Auf jeden Fall ein Stück Vorfreude: Der Aufstieg wird wird mit grandiosen Ausblicken belohnt werden.
A stairway to heaven? Certainly a touch of joyful anticipation: The ascent will be rewarded with magnificent views.

Strand, Sand, Dünen

Der fast 40 Kilometer lange Sylter Weststrand ist ein einziges Naturwunder. Der Sand ist überall hell und sauber, die Brandung immer faszinierend und das Meerwasser stets von guter Qualität. Wo man am liebsten hingeht, entscheidet sich eher nach der Nähe zur Unterkunft oder bestimmten Vorlieben: Gibt es vor Ort Gastronomie? Ist der Fußweg zum Strand sehr weit? Ist der Zugang barrierefrei? Sind Hunde zugelassen? Gibt es dort noch freie Strandkörbe? Sehr belebten Abschnitten wie in Westerland, Wenningstedt oder Kampen stehen eher ruhigere wie zwischen Rantum und Hörnum oder am Ellenbogen gegenüber. Am stets breiten Sylter Strand kann jeder seinen ganz persönlichen Platz an der Sonne finden. Auch für Naturfreude, die nicht nur Strand wollen, bietet Sylt viele Möglichkeiten. Der sinnlichste Weg zur ersten Orientierung ist der Aufstieg zur 52,5 Meter hohen Uwe-Düne in Kampen. Diese höchste natürliche Erhebung der Insel wurde nach dem Heimatdichter Uwe Jens Lornsen benannt. Hier erlebt man Sylt im 360°-Panorama: im Westen unterhalb des bis zu 30 Meter hohen Kliffs der Strand und das offene Meer, gen Norden hinter großartigen Heideflächen das Kliffende und ein weiter Blick in Richtung List, im Osten das Wattenmeer und im Süden bis Wenningstedt das Naturschutzgebiet „Dünenlandschaft auf dem Roten Kliff". Ganz Sylt liegt dem Betrachter hier zu Füßen. Ein sanfter Einstieg in das Naturerlebnis

BEACH, SAND, DUNES

At almost 40 kilometres long, the Weststrand (west beach) of Sylt is a unique natural wonder. The sand is consistently light coloured and clean, the surf always fascinating and everywhere the water is of good quality. When deciding where preferably to visit, it usually depends on the location of one's lodgings or on particular preferences: Is there gastronomy on offer? Is the beach within walking distance? Is there barrier-free access? Are dogs allowed? Are free wicker beach chairs still available? Very popular stretches of the West Beach such as in Westerland, Wenningstedt and Kampen are in contrast to more quiet locations such as between Rantum and Hörnum or on Ellenbogen land spit. On the continuously broad Sylt beach everyone can find their truly personal place in the sun. For nature lovers too, who look not only for beach life, Sylt offers many possibilities. The most sensual route for initial orientation is walking up the 52.5 metre high Uwe Dune in Kampen. This, the island's highest natural elevation, is named after Sylt's native poet Uwe Jens Lornsen. One can experience Sylt here in a 360° panorama: To the west, the beach and the open sea below the cliffs that are up to 30 metres high, looking north, behind wonderful heathlands, the end of the cliffs and a further view towards List. To the East is Wadden Sea and in the South as far as Wenningstedt there is the nature reserve of the 'dune landscape on the Red Cliff'. The whole of Sylt is at one's feet here. A softer introduction to the nature

Die Sylter Natur bietet vor allem Heide- und Dünenlandschaften. Diese aber in sehr großer Vielfalt.
Sylt's open country offers above all heathland and dune landscapes. They are to be found however in great diversity.

Sylt ist auch die gut einstündige Wanderung von Kampen aus durch die 137 Hektar große naturgeschützte Braderuper Heide und dann am Wattenmeer in Richtung Süden bis zum 15 Meter hohen Weißen Kliff. Dort am Ostufer liegt auch Braderup, das gemeinsam mit dem traditionsreichen Wenningstedt eine Gemeinde bildet. Wer will, kann noch etwas weiter bis in den kleinen Ort Munkmarsch laufen. Hier verkehrte bis zum Bau des Hindenburgdamms die wichtige Fähre nach Hoyer. Den Damm würde man erreichen, wenn man nun Richtung Osten am Watt weiterläuft. (Siehe auch Kapitel „Zwischen Marsch und Kliff"). Als Startpunkt oder für eine Rast bietet sich neben Kampen und Westerland auch Wenningstedt an. Der neu gestaltete Platz auf dem südlichen Ende des Roten Kliffs mit seiner hochmodernen breiten Holztreppe, die hier hinunter zum Strand führt, lädt zum Verweilen und Genießen ein. Viele halten den Ellenbogen, die nördlichste Ecke Sylts und damit Deutschlands für die reizvollste Gegend der ganzen Insel. Dieser Nehrungshaken nordwestlich des Ortes List ist Ziel einer zweiten Tour. Der etwa 20 Kilometer lange Fahrradweg von Westerland nach List wurde, genau wie jener in den Inselsüden nach Hörnum, überwiegend auf der Trasse der ehemaligen Inselbahn erbaut. Spätestens hinter Kampen führt die Strecke durch wenig bebautes Gelände, wo sich die Dünen- und Heidegebiete mit all ihren Düften und faszinie-

experience of Sylt is the one-hour-long hike from Kampen through the 137 hectare conservation zone of Braderup Heath and then beside Wadden Sea towards the South as far as the 15 metre high White Cliff. Here on the Eastern shore lies Braderup, which forms a community with the tradition-steeped Wenningstedt. One can walk a little further, if desired, into the small Munkmarsch village. It was here that the important ferry ran to Hoyer until the construction of the Hindenburgdamm. The dam could be reached if one walked further east on the Wadden Sea mudflats (see also the chapter 'Between marsh and cliff'). Along with Kampen and Westerland, Wenningstedt also lends itself as a starting point or to make a break. The newly designed space at the southern end of the Red Cliff with its ultra modern, wide, wooden steps, which lead down to the beach, invites one to linger and savour it all. Many consider Ellenbogen, the northernmost corner of Sylt, and thus of Germany, as the most exciting area of the whole island. This hooked spit of land northwest of List is the destination of a second tour. The circa 20 kilometre long cycle path from Westerland to List was largely built on the former island-railway line, just like the one on the South of the island to Hörnum. At the latest when passing Kampen, the line runs through largely undeveloped land, where the dunes and heathlands with all their aromas and fascinating sights and vistas can be enjoyed so close up. Those who wish to visit List should follow this line to its end. The route to Ellenbogen veers off to the left

Dänemark ist nicht weit: Baken am Ellenbogen (links) helfen den Grenzverlauf im Watt zu finden.
Denmark is not far away: Daymarkers at the Ellenbogen peninsula (left) help to determine the border demarcation in Wadden Sea.

Am Sylter Ellenbogen leben deutlich mehr Schafe als Menschen. Und die Tiere scheinen sich hier richtig wohlzufühlen.
Considerably more sheep than people live on Sylt's Ellenbogen peninsula, and the animals here appear to be really quite contented.

Je nach Tageszeit und Sonneneinstrahlung wirkt die Sylter Natur immer wieder anders und neu, doch immer faszinierend.
Depending on the time of day and amount of sunlight, time and again Sylt's nature seems different and new, but always fascinating.

renden An- und Ausblicken hautnah genießen lassen. Wer in den Ort List will, folgt dieser Trasse bis zum Ende. Der Weg zum Ellenbogen biegt hinter der Bushaltestelle Westerheide/ Blidsel nach Westen ab. Nach einer imposanten Tour westlich der riesigen, letzte Wanderdüne Deutschlands, der Sylter Sahara, erreicht man kurz hinter dem letzten Strandaufgang eine kleine Mautstation. Ab hier ist alles Privatbesitz und für Autofahrer wird eine Gebühr fällig. Die komplette Landzunge ist Naturschutzgebiet und der Besucher muss auf den erlaubten Wegen bleiben. Von der etwa fünf Kilometer langen, etwas holprigen Straße zur Ellenbogenspitze erblickt man, von ganz wenigen Gebäuden abgesehen, nur Sand, Heideflächen und ein paar Schafe. Auf manchen Fußwegen in Richtung offenes Meer spürt man, wie hoch manche Dünen hier sind. Aber so bieten sich einem auch reichlich fantastische Panoramen. Am Strand angekommen fühlt man sich an vielen Tagen wie an einem völlig unberührten Gestade, so gut verteilen sich die wenigen Menschen hier. Weitab vom sonstigen Strandbetrieb der Insel ist das Baden hier teilweise sogar verboten: Mit gefährlich hoher Geschwindigkeit vereinigt sich hier im Rhythmus der Tiden das Wasser der offenen Nordsee sprudelnd mit dem des Wattenmeeres. Auf dem Rückweg lohnt der Blick über den Königshafen. Diese wunderschön gelegene Bucht gilt als ideales Surfrevier. Schließlich kann die Tour von

just after the Westerheide/Blidsel bus stop. After this impressive tour west of Germany's last, giant shifting sand dune, Sylt's Sahara, the approach to the small toll gate to Listland, just beyond the last beach access, is reached. Everything is privately owned beyond this point and vehicle drivers are required to pay a fee. The entire spit of land is a nature reserve and the visitor must remain on the designated tracks. Apart from very few buildings, one sees only sand, heathland and a few sheep along the circa five kilometre long rather bumpy road to the tip of Ellenbogen. Along some footpaths leading to the open sea, one notices how high some of the dunes are, but they thus offer plentiful fantastic panoramas. When reaching the beach, on some days one feels like being on a quite pristine, untouched shore, so well are the few people dispersed hereabouts. Far away from the other popular beaches on the island, bathing here is however forbidden at many places: At very high speed and in rhythm with the tides, the open waters of the North Sea unite in swirling turbulence with those of Wadden Sea. On the way back one should venture a look across to Königshafen. This wonderfully situated bay ranks as an ideal windsurfing area. Finally, the trek from Westerland to Hörnum is reccommended which, depending on the paths taken, is between 20 and 24 kilometres long. Behind Westerland one soon comes to the quiet, elongated resort of Rantum. The Weststrand and Wadden Sea are at places less than 1 kilometre apart from here. After Rantum the

Bleiben Sie im Naturschutzgebiet auf den Wegen! Viele Pflanzen sind hier ebenso schön wie sensibel.
Remain on the paths in the nature reserve! Many plants are as beautiful as they are sensitive.

Um das sensible Gleichgewicht der Sylter Natur zu bewahren, dürfen manche Abschnitte der Insel gar nicht betreten werden.
In order to preserve the delicate balance of Sylt's nature, some parts of the island may not be entered at all.

Vielleicht das typischste Tier der Insel: die Möwe. Den Seevogel zu füttern, kann allerdings zu hohen Geldstrafen führen.
Perhaps the most characteristic animal of the island: The seagull. Feeding seabirds can however lead to serious fines.

Westerland nach Hörnum empfohlen, die je nach Wegstrecke zwischen 20 und 24 Kilometer lang ist. Hinter Westerland erreicht man dabei schon bald den ruhigen, lang gezogenen Urlaubsort Rantum. Hier sind Weststrand und Wattenmeer stellenweise weniger als ein Kilometer voneinander entfernt. Hinter Rantum wird das Land dann immer einsamer. Bis zur Jugendherberge am Ortseingang von Hörnum finden sich auf den etwa zehn Kilometern auch kaum noch Gebäude an der Straße – zu den wenigen Ausnahmen gehört das Jugendfreizeitheim Puan Klent. Folgt man dem Fahrrad- und Wanderweg entlang der ehemaligen Inselbahntrasse wird es noch ursprünglicher. Die oft extrem schmalen Streifen Dünen und Heide wirken fast wie in einer Miniatur und machen die Landschaft so noch intensiver erlebbar. Am Wattenmeer ist es hier noch ruhiger als nördlich des Hindenburgdamms. Das Erlebnis einer solchen Tour ins scheinbare Nirgendwo sollte der Sylt-Urlauber sich nicht entgehen lassen. Am Ziel lohnt sich auch der Besuch des Ortes Hörnum mit seinem Hafen und dem imposanten Weg um die Südspitze Odde. Von Strandspaziergängen einmal abgesehen, ist für die meisten Inseltouren das Fahrrad das Verkehrsmittel der Wahl. So sind auch größere Entfernungen kein Problem und dennoch lässt sich der Reiz der Landschaft gut erleben. Bei unerwartet ungünstigem Wetter kann man dann immer noch den Fahrradtransport am Heck der Linienbusse nutzen.

landscape becomes even more lonely. Up until the youth hostel at the entrance to the village of Hörnum there are hardly any buildings along the roughly ten kilometres of road – of the few exceptions there is the Puan Klent youth recreational facility. If one follows the cyclists' and walkers' path along the former island railway line the land displays even more of its original state. The extremely narrow strips of dunes and heathland in some parts appear as if they are in miniature and render the landscape as even more intensely perceptible. At Wadden Sea it is more tranquil here than to the North of the Hindenburg Dam. The Sylt visitor should certainly not miss the experience of such a tour into an apparent nowhere. Upon arrival it is well worth a visit to the village of Hörnum with its harbour and the beautiful trail around Odde as Sylt's southern tip is known. Apart from beach walks, for most island tours the transport mode of choice is the bicycle, where longer distances are of no consequence and in addition the charm of the landscape is best appreciated. If unexpected adverse weather occurs, one can make use of public buses which carry bicycles on a rack on the back.

Bei Hörnum endet Sylt im Süden. Hier geht es durchaus etwas ruhiger zu als in vielen anderen Orten.
Towards the south, Sylt ends at Hörnum. It is certainly somewhat more tranquil here than at many other locations.

Geschichten vom schönen Zuhause

Der Name des Einrichtungsgeschäfts Homestories wurde von Ramona Dreessen und Ralf Langmaack klug gewählt. Er lässt viele Deutungen zu, aber eine ist: Die Fantasie der Kunden wird angeregt. Beim Betrachten der schönen Dinge, der Möbel verschiedenster internationaler Hersteller, der Lampen, Stoffe, Accessoires oder Kunstgegenstände entstehen schnell kleine Geschichten vor dem inneren Auge: Momentaufnahmen eines perfekter Morgens vielleicht, an dem Körper und Geist mit dem eigenen Zuhause im Einklang sind – Wunschträume, Glücksmomente, eine Art von Homestory. „Viele Kunden suchen gar nichts Bestimmtes, kommen aber einfach gern in den Laden, um zu sehen, was wir wieder Neues haben", sagt Ramona Dreessen. – „Und manche Stammkunden, auch Urlauber, kommen auch nur zum Hallo-Sagen vorbei", ergänzt Ralf Langmaack lächelnd. Die beiden gebürtigen Sylter haben aber nicht nur einen verführerischen Laden mit großer Bandbreite und Originalität, Homestories bietet auch professionelle Planung und Umsetzung vor Ort. Dazu gehört die Beratung zu Möbeln, Tapeten, Dekoration oder Kunstobjekten ebenso wie die komplette Einrichtung von Hotelzimmern, Wohnungen oder Häusern, und das auch für fast jedes Budget. Ramona Dreessen: „Homestories steht nicht zwangsläufig für hohe Preise, aber immer für guten Geschmack und Topqualität". Nicht alles, was man für eine glückliche Homestory braucht, kann man erwerben, aber für den Rest lohnt sich ganz bestimmt ein Besuch bei Homestories.

NARRATIVES FROM A BEAUTIFUL HOME

The name of this home furnishing business, Homestories, was wisely chosen by Ramona Dreessen and Ralf Langmaack. It permits many interpretations, and one of these is: The customers' fantasy is stimulated. When observing some beautiful things, the furniture from the most varying international manufacturers, the lamps, textiles and fabrics, accessories or objets d'art, there rapidly emerge little narratives before the inner eye: snapshots of a perfect morning perhaps, when body and soul are in harmony with one's own home – subconscious yearnings and desires, moments of happiness, a kind of home-story. "Many customers are looking for nothing in particular, they are quite simply happy to come into the store in order to once again see what new things we have", says Ramona Dreessen – "and some regular customers, holiday makers too, come by just to say hello to us", adds Ralf Langmaack smiling. Both born on Sylt, they do not only have a very alluring store with a vast range and originality, Homestories also offers professional on-site planning and implementation. This of course includes advice regarding furniture, wall coverings, decoration and art objects as well as advice on completely furnishing hotel rooms, apartments and houses, and all this to suite almost every purse. Ramona Dreessen: "Homestories does not necessarily mean high prices, but always good taste and top quality". Not everything that one needs for a happy home-story can be purchased, but for all the rest, it is certainly well worth a visit to Homestories.

HOMESTORIES OHG
Ramona Dreessen und Ralf Langmaack
Andreas-Nielsen-Straße 10
25980 Sylt / OT Westerland
Telefon 046 51 / 995 27 76
mail@homestories.cc
www.homestories.cc

PIET BOON
STYLING
Ein Herz für Häuser 2

Beach BOX
Essen auf die Hand

Super Burger aus der Box

Am Ende der Käpt'n-Christiansen-Straße liegt einer der Zugänge zum Westerländer Strand. Und genau dort steht auch die Beach Box, eine kleine beliebte Burgerbude. Der Name stammt noch von dem ehemaligen Kiosk an dieser Stelle. Der einstige Küchenchef Lars Oliver Witte und seine Frau waren bereits viele Jahre in der Sylter Gastronomie erfolgreich, als sie sich 2013 entschlossen, den Laden zu pachten. Der Plan: ein wenig entschleunigen, mit einem begrenzten, aber hochwertigen Angebot das Auskommen sichern und einfach Spaß bei der Arbeit haben.Das mit dem Spaß im Job und der Qualität hat auch gut geklappt. Aber Zeit zum Aufatmen gibt es in der Beach Box selten, zumindest in der Saison. Denn die Kunden stehen Schlange, um an das authentische und originell zubereitete Essen zu gelangen. Und so wird hier am laufenden Band geschnippelt, gebraten und garniert. Verkaufsschlager ist der Cheeseburger mit zweierlei Käse, dazu natürlich meistens Pommes. Wer etwas anderes möchte, findet neben weiteren Burgersorten noch eine ganze Reihe warmer und kalter Speisen auf der Karte; Eis und Getränke gibt's natürlich auch. Alles immer zum Mitnehmen und liebevoll strandtauglich verpackt. Denn da isst es sich auch viel entspannter, wenn von hinten wieder ein paar Dutzend Beach-Box-Fans nachrücken. Budenchef Witte und sein Team werden wohl wieder bis zum Winter warten müssen, um doch noch etwas zu entschleunigen. Aber, Moment mal, war da nicht irgendwas mit Beach-Box-Glühwein in der Planung?

BEACH BOX SYLT – BURGER BUDE
Lars Oliver Witte
Käpt'n-Christiansen-Straße 42
25980 Sylt / OT Westerland

SUPER BURGERS FROM THE BOX

At the end of Käpt'n-Christiansen-Straße there is one of the entrances to Westerland Beach. And it is right here that the Beach Box can be found, a small but popular burger stall. The name comes from a former kiosk that stood here. The former chef de cuisine Lars Oliver Witte and his wife had already been successful in the Sylt gastronomy scene when they decided to lease the Box in 2013. The plan: slowing down a little, with a limited but high value selection on offer to make ends meet and simply to have fun with their work. The two ideas of having fun at work and the quality of their products worked out well, but finding time to slow down a little comes very seldom in the Beach Box, at least during the high season. Indeed, the customers form long queues to get some of the authentic and originally prepared food. Thus almost non-stop in the stall, a process of cutting and chopping, frying and garnishing continues. The big seller is the cheeseburger with two types of cheese, and naturally French fries are usually served with it. Those looking for something else will find, along with other kinds of burger, a whole selection of warm and cold dishes on the menu. Ice cream and drinks are of course also available. All of these are to-go and tenderly packed to be suitable for the beach, where it is more relaxing to recline on the sand, especially if a few dozen Beach Box fans are moving up right behind you. The stall manager Witte and his team will probably have to wait again until winter in order to slow down a little. Although, wait a minute! Wasn't there something about Beach Box glühwein being planned for the festive season?

Grün kommt weiter

Gerade vor Hotels, Restaurants, Geschäften, aber auch im privaten Bereich können schöne und repräsentative Kübelbepflanzungen eine individuelle und einladende Atmosphäre vermitteln. In der Praxis allerdings wird diese Chance, durch fehlende Zeit, mangelnde Pflanzenkenntnis oder handwerkliche Fehler oft nicht genutzt. Pflanzenpflege wird vergessen, und viele Kübel fristen eher ein trauriges Dasein. Diese Situation brachte Gartenprofi Jens Reichel 2011 auf seine Idee: Den grünen Daumen zum Mieten! – Pflanzkübelservice GRUEN+. Das Auswechseln der Bepflanzung durfte jedoch nur wenig Zeit in Anspruch nehmen. Viele Geschäftsleute wollen keine Handwerker, die sich lange aufhalten, womöglich Schmutz machen und die Kunden beim Urlaubmachen stören. Reichels Lösung: Die Kübelbepflanzung befindet sich in mobilen Einsätzen, die innerhalb weniger Minuten getauscht werden. Die Idee kam gut an, und so konnte der Pflanzkübelservice eine begeisterte Stammkundschaft quer über die Insel gewinnen. Außer den beliebten Blütenarrangements, die GRUEN+ regelmäßig alle fünf bis sechs Wochen erneuert, werden auch Saison- und Fixbepflanzungen realisiert sowie – etwa für Hochzeiten oder Geschäftseröffnungen – individuelle Pflanzendekorationen gestaltet. Neben dem Komplettservice, der Gießen, Düngen und Pflege der Bepflanzung beinhaltet, bietet Reichel noch weitere Dienstleistungen rund um das Thema „Grün plus" an. Seine Kunden merken schnell, dass er seine kreative Leidenschaft zum Beruf gemacht hat.

GREEN MOVES FORWARD

In particular in front of hotels, restaurants, businesses, but also in the private sector, beautiful and representative plant tubs can impart an individual and inviting atmosphere. In practice however, this chance is often not taken advantage of, due to a lack of time, insufficient knowledge of plants or simple manual mistakes. The care of plants is forgotten, and many plant tubs spend a rather sad, withered life. In 2011 this situation inspired garden expert Jens Reichel to his concept: To put his green fingers up for rental! – plant tub service GRUEN+. Interchanging the plants should only take up a little time. Many business people do not need tradesmen who are perhaps in the way or cause a delay, maybe creating a mess and disturbing the customers on their holiday. Reichel's solution was simple: As part of a mobile service the plant tubs can be exchanged in a matter of minutes. The concept was well received, and thus the plant tub service was able to win over a delighted body of regular customers right around the island. Apart from the much loved flower arrangements, which GRUEN+ regularly replaced every five to six weeks, seasonal and semi-permanent pot plants were also made available, as well as – for instance for weddings or opening events for new businesses – individual plant decorations being specifically designed. Alongside the complete service which, aside from the plant-care itself, includes watering and fertilising, Reichel provides even more services in the overall context of the topic 'Grün plus'. His customers soon realise that he has turned his creative passion into a profession.

GRUEN+/SYLT
Inhaber: Jens Reichel
Kollundweg 20
25980 Sylt / OT Westerland
Telefon 01 72 / 860 11 18
info@gruenplus-sylt.de
www.gruenplus-sylt.de

Noch etwas zu verzollen?

Das Alte Zollhaus Westerland in der Boysenstraße ist ein schön restaurierter Backsteinbau aus dem frühen 20. Jahrhundert. Es diente noch bis 1977 tatsächlich als Zollamt, bis es 2011 durch das Restaurant Altes Zollhaus zu neuer Bekanntheit gelangte. 2014 übernahm die Familie Suchy das gehobene Speiserestaurant. Seitdem ist das Alte Zollhaus beliebtes Ziel aller Freunde stimmungsvoller Atmosphäre und guten Essens. Suchy, der mit seiner Firma Höpershof Profi in Sachen geschmackvoller Raumgestaltung ist, hat hier gemeinsam mit seinem Service- und Küchenteam einen Ort geschaffen, an dem sich niemand gesellschaftlichem Stress aussetzen muss und dennoch gehobene Gastronomie genießen kann: zum Beispiel klassische Fisch- und Fleischgerichte, die durch Kombination mit asiatischen Elementen ein überraschendes Cross-over-Flair erhalten, das experimentierfreudigen Gästen Spaß macht, ohne den traditionellen Gast abzuschrecken. Das Alte Zollhaus lässt sich kaum verfehlen: Die Fackeln am Eingang flackern einladend, und die stimmungsvoll eingedeckte Holzterrasse rund um die alte Linde wirkt stets wie für ein Fest geschmückt. Viele Passanten halten hier kurz inne, als würden sie sich am liebsten gleich dazusetzen. Das steht auch jedem frei, nur in der Saison wird um rechtzeitige Reservierung gebeten. Der Gastraum des Restaurants bietet maximal 45 Personen Platz und die malerische Holzterrasse ist so etwas wie eine heiß begehrte Loge an den belebten Wegen Westerlands.

ANYTHING ELSE TO DECLARE?

The Altes Zollhaus (old customs house) in Westerland in Boysenstraße is a beautifully restored red-brick building from the early 20th century. It did indeed still serve as a customs office right up to 1977, and then gained new prominence in 2011 as Restaurant Altes Zollhaus. In 2014 the Suchy family took over this haute cuisine eating-house. Since then it has become a favourite destination for all friends of a welcoming, emotional atmosphere and good food. Suchy, who with his Höpershof company is a professional in matters of tasteful interior design, and together with his service and kitchen staff here, has created a locale where no-one is exposed to societal stress and can nevertheless enjoy high-end gastronomy: for example classic fish and meat dishes which, in combination with Asian elements, take on a surprising crossover flair, which is a pleasure for adventuresome guests, without scaring off the more traditional ones. The Altes Zollhaus is hard to miss: The flaming torches at the entrance invitingly shimmer, and the mood-filled atmosphere of the festively set wooden terrace right around the old lime tree seems to be decorated for a celebration. Many passers by stop for a moment here and reflect, as though they would prefer to sit down at once and join in, which anyone is free to do of course; only in the peak season is a timely reservation requested. The seating area within has places for a maximum of 45 persons and the picturesque wooden terrace is somewhat like a much sought-after theatre box on the popular pathways of Westerland.

RESTAURANT ALTES ZOLLHAUS SYLT GMBH
Geschäftsführer: Oliver Suchy
Boysenstraße 18
25980 Sylt / OT Westerland
Telefon: 046 51 / 44 94 43
info@altes-zollhaus-sylt.de
www.altes-zollhaus-sylt.de

Vom Reiz schöner Häuser

Nicht jeder liebt es, in modernen Stahl- und Glasgebäuden zu wohnen, auch wenn sie noch so luxuriös eingerichtet sind. Mancher mag auch einfach die hochwertige und oft auch natürlichere Art, in der man vor hundert Jahren gebaut hat. Und vielleicht gerade im Sylt-Urlaub werden wieder andere von einer Art romantischer Sehnsucht nach der guten alten Bäder-Zeit erfasst, auch da taugt ein altes Haus viel besser zum Feriendomizil als ein Neubau. Wer das möchte und dennoch nicht auf modernsten Komfort verzichten will, für den ist das Hotel Sylter Zollhaus in der Boysenstraße 16 in Westerland ideal. Es bietet das Beste beider Welten, der guten alten und der bequemen modernen Zeit. Nach sorgfältiger Renovierung und Restaurierung wurde das kleine Hotel im Mai 2016 eröffnet. Die sieben Luxussuiten auf drei Etagen können alle problemlos mit dem Fahrstuhl erreicht werden. Jede von ihnen hat mindestens 35 Quadratmeter Wohnfläche, einen Kamin und eine komfortable Einrichtung im Stil des Höpershof. Zum Wellnessbereich gelangt man durch einen unterirdischen Verbindungsgang. Das Frühstück und auf Wunsch das Abendessen werden gleich nebenan im beliebten Restaurant Altes Zollhaus serviert. Der Familienbetrieb Höpershof ist seit 2006 unter anderem erfolgreich in der Vermietung exklusiver Ferienwohnungen auf Sylt. Mit dem Sylter Zollhaus hat man nun auch ein perfektes Angebot für Gäste geschaffen, die lieber in einem Hotel wohnen, zum Beispiel weil sie nur wenige Tage bleiben.

THE ALLURE OF BEAUTIFUL HOUSES

Not everyone enjoys living in modern steel and glass buildings, even if they are luxuriously furnished. Some simply prefer the high-quality, and often also the more natural form, which was used in construction one hundred years ago. And perhaps particularly when on holiday on Sylt, others will be seized by a kind of romantic desire for those good old bathing times. In such moments, an old house is much more suitable as holiday accommodation than a new building. For those who prefer such a holiday but who will not forego the most modern comfort, then the Hotel Sylter Zollhaus (customs house) in Boysenstraße 16 in Westerland is ideal. It offers the best of both worlds, the good old, and the comfortable modern times. After careful renovation and restoration, this small hotel was opened in May 2016. The seven luxury suites on three floors can all easily be reached by lift. They all have at least 35 square metres of living space, a real-fire hearth and comfortable furnishing in Höpershof style. An underground connecting tunnel provides access to the wellness area. Breakfast, and where desired, dinner is served right next door in the popular Restaurant Altes Zollhaus. Among other enterprises the Höpershof family business has been successfully letting exclusive holiday apartments on Sylt since 2006. With the Sylt Zollhaus they have now created a perfect opportunity for guests who prefer to live in a hotel, for instance because they will only be staying for a few days.

HOTEL SYLTER ZOLLHAUS
HÖPERSHOF GMBH
Geschäftsführerin: Susanne Kreuzberg-Suchy
Boysenstraße 16
25980 Sylt / OT Westerland
Telefon 0 46 51 / 66 95
info@hoepershof-sylt.de
www.galeria-hoepershof.de/ferienwohnungen/hotel-sylter-zollhaus.php

STEFFI-MODEN
H A GÜLCHER
NEW

Modetrends mit Leidenschaft

Die Friedrichstraße in Westerland gehört sicherlich zu den meistbesuchten Meilen der Insel. Und es gibt nicht wenige Urlauber, die sich hier besonders über Geschäfte freuen, die es schon in ihrer Kindheit gab. Kontinuität schafft Vertrauen, und so gehört ein Besuch bei Steffi-Moden wie eh und je zum Pflichtprogramm einer Shoppingtour. In das 300 Quadratmeter große Modehaus in bester Lage kommen die Kunden oft schon in der dritten Generation. Jeder kennt die nicht enden wollende Schaufenstergalerie an der Ecke Friedrichstraße/Elisabethstraße. Auf Sylt ist das Geschäft für sportive Damen- und Herrenmode bereits seit 1957 erfolgreich. Der bereits 1919 gegründete Hamburger Familienbetrieb ist bis heute auch in der Hansestadt aktiv. Viele modische Impulse und Trends gehen bis heute von hier aus. Besonders beliebt bei den Kunden sind die hauseigenen Modelle, die von besten Herstellern im guten Preis-Leistungs-Verhältnis speziell für Steffi-Moden produziert werden. Neben diesen Eigenmarken führt das Haus – zum großen Teil exklusiv auf der Insel – unter anderem Modelle von Bogner über Cambio bis hin zu Lieblingsstück. Die Verkaufsabteilung ist unermüdlich in den internationalen Modemetropolen auf der Suche nach dem Besonderen. Die Accessoires aus Paris und Mailand werden fast wöchentlich neu disponiert. Geschulte, liebenswerte Verkaufsberater und eine gute Atmosphäre machen den Besuch bei Steffi-Moden immer wieder zu einem Einkaufserlebnis der besonderen Klasse.

FASHION TRENDS WITH A PASSION

Friedrichstraße in Westerland certainly belongs to the most visited stretches of the island, and it's not just a few visitors who are pleased to see all these stores which were here in their childhood. Continuity creates trust, and so a visit to Steffi-Moden is as ever, part of the mandatory programme in a shopping tour. In this 300 square metre fashion house in a prime location, customers often come here in their third generation. Everyone knows the seemingly never-ending window gallery at the corner of Friedrichstraße and Elisabethstraße. This women's and men's sportive fashions store on Sylt has been successful from as early as 1957. The family business, initially founded as early as 1919 in Hamburg is still in business here today. Many fashion impulses and trends still originate from this fashion house today. Especially popular among the customers are the own-brand designs, which are produced by the best manufacturers especially for Steffi-Moden at good value for money. Along with these in-house labels, the company offers – to a large extent exclusively on the island – articles from Bogner to Cambio to Lieblingsstück among others. The sales department is untiring in the international fashion metropolises in search of that something special. The accessories from Paris and Milan are planned and scheduled anew almost weekly. Well trained, amiable sales advisors and a good atmosphere turn a visit to Steffi-Moden time and again into a shopping experience in a class of its own.

STEFFI-MODEN
H. A. Gülcher GmbH
Friedrichstraße 35
25980 Sylt / OT Westerland
Telefon 046 51 / 231 22
info@steffi-moden.de
www.steffi-moden.de

Eine Familie sagt: „hello beauty"

Eine neue Filiale bedeutet gerade für einen mittelständischen Betrieb immer eine große Herausforderung. Das seit 1995 erfolgreiche Familienunternehmen Akzente aus Baden-Württemberg hat es gewagt: Eine Beautywelt mit rund 150 Quadratmetern auf zwei Etagen bereichert seit 2016 die Westerländer Einkaufsmeile. Stefanie Renchen, Juniorchefin des Unternehmens, und ihre Familie haben die Chance, sich in Westerland niederzulassen, sehr gern ergriffen. Nicht nur, weil es ein interessanter Markt ist, sondern auch, weil sie privat immer schon große Sylt-Fans waren. „Wir kommen mit vielen frischen Ideen", sagt Stefanie Renchen, „unsere inspirierende Beautywelt begeistert mit ausgewählten Nischenmarken und bekannten Designerbrands im Duft-, Pflege- und Make-up-Bereich, trendigen Home- und Modeaccessoires sowie kreativen Geschenkideen." In der Akzente-Beautylounge im Obergeschoss stehen zudem mehrere Räume für individuelle Kosmetikberatungen und kosmetische Spezialbehandlungen bereit. Ein gutes Angebot, gerade auch für Sylt-Urlauber, die im Alltag manchmal nicht die Zeit dafür finden. „Bei uns steht der Mensch im Mittelpunkt, sowohl der Kunde als auch der Mitarbeiter, alle sollen sich hier wohlfühlen", erläutert die Juniorchefin die Unternehmensphilosophie und fährt fort: „Schönheit ist für uns ein Teil des Lebensgefühls, das Freude und Leidenschaft weckt. Das möchten wir an unsere Kunden weitergeben und durch unsere Beratung neue Akzente setzen, die das ganze Leben schöner machen."

A FAMILY SAYS: "HELLO BEAUTY"

Particularly for a medium-sized company, a new subsidiary store always brings with it a new challenge. Akzente, a family business from Baden-Württemberg and successful since 1995, took up the challenge: A beauty centre with about 150 square metres on two floors has been enhancing the Westerland shopping mile since 2016.
Stefanie Renchen, the company's junior manager, and her family were very happy to take the chance to move to and live in Westerland. Not only because it is an interesting market, but also because in their private lives they had always been big fans of Sylt. "We have brought with us many fresh ideas", says Stefanie Renchen, "our inspirational beauty centre enthusiastically delights our clientele with selected niche brands and well-known designer brands in the fragrance, care and make-up categories, trendy home and fashion accessories as well as creative gift ideas". In the Akzente beauty lounge on the upper floor there are in addition several rooms available for individual cosmetic consultation and advice, and special cosmetic treatments. A good opportunity, for Sylt holiday makers as well, who sometimes do not find the time for beauty centres in their everyday lives. "For us here, the individual is the main focus, the customer as well as the member of our staff, all of them should feel comfortable here", says the junior manager, outlining the company philosophy, and continues: "Beauty is for us a part of an attitude towards life that awakens joy and passion. This is what we wish to impart to our customers and to bring out new accents through our advice that make one's whole life more beautiful."

AKZENTE – PARFÜMERIE & BEAUTY
Friedrichstraße 29–31
25980 Sylt / OT Westerland
Telefon 046 51 / 835 02 50
service@akzenteplus.de
www.akzenteplus.de

la prairie
la prairie
la prairie
MBR
MBR
MBR

Blühende Kreativität

Was ist die Alte Wäscherei in Westerland? Ein Blumenladen, in dem es manchmal Bademoden gibt, oder ein Einrichtungsgeschäft, in dem man auch Blumen bekommt? – Sie ist all das, noch viel mehr und nichts von alldem, und morgen kann es schon wieder ganz anders sein. Genau das ist die Konzeptidee: Räume mit wechselnden Inhalten. Das Publikum soll erleben, entdecken, kreativ werden, assoziieren, sich in Sachen verlieben und natürlich auch gern etwas kaufen. Aber auch Besucher, die sich nur umschauen wollen, sind hier absolut erwünscht. Die Blumen waren anfangs nur als Türöffner gedacht, als Dekoration für alte und neue Designermöbel, originelle Industrieobjekte, handgefertigten Schmuck und weitere Dinge, die man wohl nirgendwo sonst auf Sylt bekommen kann. Aber inzwischen sind so viele Einheimische, Touristen, Hoteliers und Hochzeitspaare zu Fans dieses etwas anderen Blumenladens geworden, dass man in der Alten Wäscherei nun doch immer Blumen bekommt. Aber es kann doch passieren, dass die Rosen, die man eigentlich wollte, gerade nicht zu haben sind. Stattdessen stehen aber vielleicht funky Nelken auf einem schönen Designertischchen und kurzerhand kauft man einfach beides. Genau deswegen lohnt es sich, öfter hier zu sein, ganz in der Nähe des Bahnhofs Westerland, dort, wo die Insel wohl am urbansten und vielleicht am untypischsten ist. Haben die Ladeninhaber eigentlich noch irgendwas dazu zu sagen? Ja, zwei Sätze: „Kommt einfach vorbei! Schönen Gruß von Svea und Johannes."

ALTE WÄSCHEREI
Kirchenweg 9
25980 Sylt / OT Westerland
Telefon 046 51 / 835 20 20
www.altewaescherei.com

BLOSSOMING CREATIVITY

What is the Alte Wäscherei (old laundry) in Westerland? A florist's shop, in which there are sometimes bathing costumes too, or a home furnishing store, where one can also buy flowers? – It is all of these, but much more, and none of these, and tomorrow it could be something quite different. This is exactly the idea of the concept: Spaces with changing content. The clientele should experience, discover, become creative, connect, fall in love with things, and of course be glad to buy something as well. But also visitors who wish only to look around are very welcome here too. At the beginning, the flowers were only meant to be a foot-in-the-door, as decoration for old and new designer furniture, original industrial objects, handcrafted jewellery and other things which one could not get anywhere else on Sylt. However, so many locals, tourists, hoteliers and bridal couples have meanwhile become fans of this somewhat offbeat flower shop, that one can now indeed still find flowers in the Alte Wäscherei. Although it could be that the roses that were actually hoped for are presently unavailable. Instead perhaps there are some funky carnations set upon a beautiful little designer table and in no time at all one has simply bought both. Precisely for this reason it is worth coming here more often, very near Westerland station where the island is at its most urban and perhaps also at its most unusual. Have the shop owners actually got anything else to add? Yes, two things: "Simply come and visit us! Best regards from Svea and Johannes."

Kleiner Bruder – großer Spaß

Menschen wie Enrico Schulze sind echte Originale – und somit selten. Das ist auch ein Grund dafür, dass man Abende in seiner Gin-Bar, dem Kleinen Bruder in Westerland, nicht so schnell vergisst. Die stets gute Laune des Wahlsylters und Gastronomieprofis führt selbst ohne Hochprozentiges bei den meisten Gästen dazu, dass sie den Laden in besserer Stimmung verlassen, als sie ihn betreten haben. Es gibt aber mindestens noch einen weiteren Grund, warum Enrico schon nach kurzer Zeit – er hat erst 2015 eröffnet – so viel Erfolg haben konnte. In Westerland gibt es zwar viele gute Restaurants, aber Nachtschwärmer haben wenig Auswahl, wenn sie zu ihrem Drink noch eine besondere Atmosphäre suchen. Nicht jeder will da auf irgendeine Kneipe oder die Hotelbar zurückgreifen. Der Kleine Bruder ist fast immer gut gefüllt, aber der Wirt und seine Kollegen kümmern sich um jeden netten Gast gleich herzlich, egal, ob Tourist oder Sylter, Arm oder Reich, Alt oder Jung, Mann oder Frau – und egal auch, welchem Geschlecht sie oder er sich zugeneigt fühlt. Und die Gäste kommen gern, in einer guten Mischung, und das ist mindestens fünf Nächte die Woche möglich, open end! Enrico, der Paradiesvogel der Insel, den man durchaus auch mal auf High Heels in der Fußgängerzone antreffen kann, bringt es auf eine einfache Formel: „Ich habe mir einen Traum erfüllt, ich liebe Sylt, ich bin glücklich mit dem Kleinen Bruder und meinen Gästen und möchte, dass jeder, der zu mir kommt, eine tolle Zeit hat."

KLEINER BRUDER – A GREAT PLEASURE

People such as Enrico Schulze are real originals – and thus seldom. This is also a reason why evenings spent in his gin bar – Kleiner Bruder (little brother) in Westerland – are not so soon forgotten. The constant good humour of this Sylt-resident-by-choice and gastronomy pro leads most guests to be in a better mood when leaving the locale than when they arrived, even without potent spirits. There is however at least one further reason why Enrico, even after only a short time – he only opened in 2015 – could have so much success. In Westerland there are indeed many good restaurants, but nighthawks have little choice if they seek a special atmosphere with their drinks. Not everyone will resort to whatever pub or hotel bar. Kleine Bruder is almost always well filled, but the landlord and his colleagues look after every friendly guest equally heartily, no matter whether tourist or Sylt native, rich or poor, old or young, man or woman – and regardless also, to which gender he or she is inclined. And the guests gladly come here, in a good mixture, and this is usually possible five nights each week, open-end! Enrico, the island's bird of paradise, who one can by all means sometimes find in the pedestrian zone in high heels, offers a very straightforward reason: "I have realised a dream, I love Sylt, I am happy with Kleinen Bruder and my guests, and I hope that everyone who comes to me has a good time."

KLEINER BRUDER – BAR LOUNGE
Enrico Schulze
Bötticherstraße 3
25980 Sylt / OT Westerland
Telefon 046 51 / 804 98 74
willkommen@kleinerbruder.net
www.kleinerbruder.net

Leicht geneigt, doch fest entschlossen: Die „Reisenden im Wind" begrüßen am Westerländer Bahnhof alle Neuankömmlinge.
Leaning slightly, but quite resolved: The 'Travellers in the Wind' greet all new arrivals at Westerland station.

Erlebnis, Spaß und schöne Sachen

Was bietet Sylt eigentlich jenseits von Strandleben, aktivem Naturerlebnis und toller Gastronomie? – Auch hier ist die Insel eine gute Wahl, denn es findet sich ein wirklich breites Angebot für jeden Geschmack. Dabei ist es egal, in welchem der zwölf Urlaubsorte man wohnt, denn dank der guten Busverbindungen und der drei Bahnhöfe der Insel gelangt man auch ohne Auto entspannt und zügig überallhin. Für den eigenen Pkw finden sich ausreichend Parkplätze. Wer shoppen will, wird Westerland mit seinen erstaunlich zahlreichen Geschäften lieben. In den Fußgängerzonen von Strandstraße und Friedrichstraße sowie vielen belebten Nebenstraßen lässt sich von Büchern bis zu Süßwaren, vom Spielzeug bis zur Sporttasche, vom Blumenstrauß bis zum Kaschmirschal, vom Radio bis zum Parfüm sowie bei jeglicher Art Kleidung für jeden Geschmack und Geldbeutel alles finden. Aber auch eine Shopping-Tour in den Norden der Insel, nach List, kann sich lohnen: Hier wird das Angebot an Kleidung, Möbeln, Andenken und vielen weiteren Dingen inzwischen von Jahr zu Jahr vielfältiger. Das gilt nicht nur für den Platz am Hafen bei der Tonnenhalle, sondern auch entlang von Listland- und Hafenstraße, wo voraussichtlich 2017 das neue große Einkaufszentrum, der Lister Markt, eröffnen wird. Auch in den Geschäften Wenningstedts und den anderen Orten kann der Sylter Gast na-

ADVENTURE, FUN AND LOVELY THINGS

What is it that Sylt can offer beyond beach life, active nature experiences and good gastronomy? Even here the island is a good choice due to the wide range of offers to suit every taste, and at the same time it is no matter in which of the twelve resorts one stays, because thanks to the good bus connections and Sylt's three railway stations one is able to relaxingly and rapidly get right around the the island without a car. There are nevertheless ample parking spaces for private cars. Those who enjoy shopping will love Westerland with its surprisingly numerous stores. In the pedestrian zones in Strandstraße and Friedrichstraße as well as in the many popular side streets much can be found, from books to candy, from toys to sports bags, from flower bouquets to cashmere scarves, from radios to perfumes as well as every type of clothing for every imaginable taste and pocket. However, a shopping trip to the island's North, to List, can also be worthwhile: Here the selection of clothes, furniture, souvenirs and many other things is meanwhile expanding annually. This is not only true for the square at the harbour beside the old Tonnenhalle, but also along Listlandstraße and Hafenstraße, where the new large shopping centre, List Market, is expected to be open in 2017. In Wenningstedt's stores as well, and in other locations as well, the Sylt visitor can of course find his or her shopping desires. Especially for admirers of high-class clothing and

Solche Bäderarchitektur ist in Westerland eher selten zu finden. Letztlich zählt der Blick aufs Meer.
Such spa architecture is usually difficult to come across in Westerland. It is ultimately the view out to sea that counts.

türlich sein Shopping-Glück finden. Gerade auch für Freunde hochwertiger Kleidung und erlesenen Schmucks lohnen sich in jedem Fall die Wege nach Keitum und Kampen. Für Erholung und Spaß ist das erst 2015 modernisierte Westerländer Freizeitbad Sylter Welle mit seinem großen Wellnessbereich die erste Adresse der Insel. Bei jedem Wetter können Jung und Alt leicht bekleidet den Blick auf Strand und Meer wagen, ohne dass es je langweilig oder kalt wird. Wer lieber etwas für den Kopf tun möchte sollte neben den Heimatmuseen in Kei-tum auch die Natur-Erlebniszentren der Insel kennen: Von den Naturgewalten in List über das Naturzentrum Braderup bis hin zur Arche Wattenmeer in der ehemaligen Hörnumer Kirche lässt sich anschaulich viel zu den Themen Meer, Klima, Insel, Tiere und Pflanzen lernen. Auch ein Besuch im Aquarium Westerland oder Ausflüge in die Vogelkojen oder in den Tierpark Tinnum machen Spaß. Regelmäßige Veranstaltungen von Lesungen über Comedy bis hin zu Konzerten aller Sparten – zum Beispiel im Kursaal[3] in Wenningstedt oder im Meerkabarett in Rantum – runden das Angebot ab. Und bereits ab dem Nachmittag zeigt das Westerländer Kino internationale Filme für jeden Geschmack und jede Altersklasse. Und so kann der Tag auf Sylt auch ganz ohne Strandaufenthalt sehr schön zu Ende gehen.

select jewellery, a trip to Keitum and Kampen would certainly be worthwhile. For relaxation and fun, the recently modernised (2015) Sylter Welle leisure pool in Westerland with its large wellness area would be the first place to visit on the island. In all weathers, lightly dressed, young and old can hazard a chance at the view out to the beach and across the sea, without becoming bored or cold. Along with the local-heritage museums in Keitum, those who wish to find some food for the brain should also visit the natural interactive discovery centres on the island: From the 'forces of nature' in List and the Naturzentrum Braderup to the Arche Wattenmeer (ark of Wadden Sea) in the former Hörnum church, everywhere clearly displayed, there is much to learn of topics such as the sea, climate, islands, animals and plants. A visit to the aquarium in Westerland or trips to the Vogelkojen nature reserve and the zoological gardens in Tinnum are much fun too. Regular events such as readings, comedy and concerts of every musical genre – for example in the Kursaal[3] in Wenningstedt, as well as in the Meerkabarett in Rantum – round off the island's indoor prospects. Early afternoon matinée marks the beginning of films shown on the multiple screens of the Westerland theatre. International films to suit every taste and every age group can be seen here. And thus another day on Sylt without any beach visit can be brought to a happy conclusion.

Kunst und Weitblick am Kliff in Wenningstedt oder ein kleiner Ausritt am Strand? Sie haben die Wahl.
Art and vision on the cliff in Wenningstedt, or a brief ride along the beach? You have the choice.

Vor lauter Strand vergisst man fast, dass Sylt auch nette Häfen hat. Zum Beispiele in List gibt es viel Hafenatmosphäre.
With so many stretches of beach, one almost forgets that Sylt also has nice harbours. In List for instance there is much harbour atmosphere.

Ein Hauch Italien im Friesenhaus

Nur wenige Hundert Meter trennen in Rantum die beiden Gestade Sylts. Der Urlauber kann mühelos zum Baden an den Sandstrand gehen und abends zum Entspannen ans stille Watt.
Als Gast des Hotels Watthof sitzt man hier in der ersten Reihe: Die zehn individuell und dezent luxuriös gestalteten Hotelzimmer und Suiten des Friesenhauses sind allesamt auf das Wattenmeer ausgerichtet, ebenso wie der schöne Frühstücksraum mit seiner Terrasse. Neben einem Wellnessbereich gehören auch ein hoteleigener Mietwagen sowie Leihfahrräder und E-Bikes zum Angebot. Nach dem Motto „Hier wird der Gast verwöhnt" werden in dem Familienbetrieb jederzeit gern individuelle Wünsche berücksichtigt. Nicht ohne Grund nennen die Gäste immer wieder das Frühstück des Watthofs als besonderes Highlight: Eine große Auswahl an frischen Brötchen und Brot, italienischen Kaffees und erlesenen Teesorten wird durch kleine, frisch zubereitete warme Speisen ergänzt. Zudem importiert der Watthof seit vielen Jahren exklusive Spezialitäten direkt aus Italien: Unter diversen Käsevariationen, erlesenen Schinken- und Salamisorten sowie vielfältigen Frucht- und Nussaufstrichen entdeckt so mancher Urlauber eine neue Lieblingsspeise. Auch Liebhaber guter Weine und Spirituosen können aus einem großen Angebot wählen. Bei einem guten Tropfen und netten Gesprächen klingt dann der Abend am Meer genussvoll aus. Entspannung am Watt und mitten in der Natur – das ist der Watthof.

A TOUCH OF ITALY IN A FRISIAN HOUSE

In Rantum only a few hundred metres separate Sylt's two opposite shores. The holidaymaker can quite easily go bathing on the sandy beach and in the evening to relax walk over to the tranquillity of the Wadden Sea mudflats. As a guest at the Hotel Watthof you can sit here with a front-row seat: The individual and subtly luxurious design of the ten hotel rooms and suites of this Frisian house are all facing across the tidal mudflats, including the beautiful breakfast room with its terrace. Along with a wellness area, there is also the hotel's own hire car as well as rental bikes and e-bikes available. According to the motto "Our guests shall be pampered" individual desires in this family business will be gladly considered at all times. Not without good reason do the guests continue to mention the breakfast of the Watthof as a special highlight: A large selection of bread and bread rolls, Italian coffees and selected teas are complemented by small, freshly cooked warm dishes. In addition, for many years the Watthof has imported exclusive specialities directly from Italy: Among various types of cheese, carefully selected hams and salamis as well as numerous fruit and nut spreads, some of our holiday guests even discover a new favourite dish. Connoisseurs of good wines and spirits can choose from a large selection. Sipping a fine wine or other drink, and perhaps with an entertaining discussion, the evening beside the sea can come to its pleasing close. Relaxation at Wadden Sea and in the midst of nature – this is the Watthof.

HOTEL WATTHOF
Raanwai 42
25980 Sylt / OT Rantum
Telefon 046 51 / 80 20
info@watthof.de
www.watthof.de

Wohlfühlen wie im Süden

Mit Shorts und Strandtasche wirklich gut essen gehen? Guckt da vielleicht jemand komisch? – Solche Gedanken kann man sich auf dem Weg zum Restaurant Coast in Rantum sparen. „Wir wollen eine ungezwungene Atmosphäre wie sie in südlichen Ländern üblich ist. Dort kommt auch jeder, wie er ist, und am besten gleich mit der ganzen Familie", sagt Jan Hendrik Rose, der gemeinsam mit seiner Frau auch das Hotel Duene gegenüber betreibt. Was die Einrichtung betrifft, dürfte allerdings halb Südeuropa neidisch sein auf Roses Restaurant. Der stilechte Neubau mit Reetdach ist mit einladend hellen Holzmöbeln im zeitgemäßen Beach-Look eingerichtet – international, unkompliziert und in bester Qualität. Das 2015 eröffnete Coast bietet Frühstück und Abendessen zu angemessenen Preisen und auch nach 22 Uhr noch eine gut sortierte Bar. Die Speisekarte ist kompakt, aber hochwertig, mit einem Schwerpunkt auf perfekt zubereiteten Fleischgerichten. Die umfangreiche Weinauswahl und verschiedene Craft-Biere helfen beim stilvollen Durstlöschen. „Bei uns kann ein Gast einfach nur einen Burger bestellen oder auf einen Drink vorbeikommen", betont Rose, „aber unsere Spitzenköche bereiten auch Vier-Gänge-Menüs auf höchstem Niveau. Dabei legen wir immer Wert auf frische saisonale Produkte der Region." Im Hochsommer empfiehlt sich allerdings eine Reservierung, denn dann kann es trotz großer Terrasse schon mal so richtig voll werden im Coast – eben ganz wie in der Lieblingsosteria!

FEELING GOOD, LIKE DOWN SOUTH

With shorts and a beach bag, dining out really well? Maybe you'll get a few stares? One can forget such thoughts on the way to Restaurant Coast in Rantum. "We want an informal atmosphere as is common in countries further south where everyone comes along just as they are, and preferably with the whole family", says Jan Hendrik Rose, who together with his wife also runs "Hotel Duene" right opposite. As far as the furnishings are concerned, half of Southern Europe would certainly be envious of Rose's Restaurant. The original-style new building with thatched roof is equipped with invitingly light, wooden furniture in contemporary beach look – international, uncomplicated and to the highest quality. Opened in 2015, Coast offers breakfast and dinner at reasonable prices, and also even after 10pm a well-stocked bar. The menu is compact yet high-grade, with a focus on perfectly prepared meat dishes. The extensive choice of wines and various craft beers stylishly help out with thirst-quenching. "A guest can simply order a burger here or just call by for a drink", Rose points out, "but our top chefs prepare four course meals of the highest quality. At the same time we also attach great importance to fresh, seasonal, local produce." In midsummer however, a reservation is recommended, because then, despite a large terrace, it really can become full in Coast. Precisely – just like in one's favourite osteria!

RESTAURANT COAST
Familie Rose
Stiindeelke 2
25980 Sylt / OT Rantum
Telefon 046 51 / 15 51
info@restaurant-coast.de
www.restaurant-coast.de

Urlaubsspaß am Rantumbecken

Gerade Familien schätzen das ruhige Rantum mit seiner guten Anbindung an Westerland und andere Gegenden der Insel. Zwischen Rantumbecken, Heide und Wald ist unter dem Namen Dorfhotel Sylt vor ein paar Jahren fast so etwas wie ein neuer Ortsteil Rantums entstanden. Das Unternehmen TUI errichtete hier Ferienhäuser mit insgesamt 159 Ein- und Zweizimmerappartements, dazu ein Hotelgebäude mit Rezeption, Tagungsräumen, einer Bar, zwei Restaurants sowie das moderne Dorfhotel Spa. Das Dorfhotel-Konzept „Im Appartement wohnen – Hotelkomfort genießen" ist nicht nur bei Familien beliebt. Zwangloser Urlaub in der Ferienwohnung wird durch praktische Hotelservices ergänzt. Der Gast entscheidet ganz individuell, wie oft gereinigt wird, wann er frische Handtücher braucht, ob Kinderbetreuung kurzfristig benötig wird, wann er im Hotelrestaurant isst, wann ein Lieferdienst oder ein Sport- und Freizeitangebot gebucht wird. Und so zahlt auch jeder immer nur für den Luxus, den er auch wirklich haben will. Die Atmosphäre auf dem Gelände gleicht tatsächlich der in einem echten Dorf: Es gibt einen Marktplatz, mehrere Sport- und Spielplätze, Grill- und Sitzecken, Dorfladen und Fahrradverleih und sogar einen Kinder- und Jugendklub. Auf diese Weise ergänzt das Dorfhotel auch die Vorzüge des Ortes Rantums, zumal viele Angebote, wie etwa Dorfladen oder Spa für jeden zur Verfügung stehen. So schön kann das Dorfleben sein und so entspannt ein Urlaub im Dorfhotel Sylt.

HOLIDAY FUN AT RANTUM BASIN

Families in particular appreciate calm, tranquil Rantum with its good connections to Westerland and other areas of the island. Emerging only a few years ago and going by the name Dorfhotel Sylt (village-hotel Sylt), it is situated between Rantum Basin, heathland and woods and it has become something of a new district of Rantum. The TUI tourism company constructed holiday homes here with a total of 159 one and two bedroom apartments, including a hotel building with reception, conference rooms, a bar, two restaurants, as well as the modern Dorfhotel Spa. The Dorfhotel concept "stay in an apartment – enjoy hotel comfort" is not only popular with families. An informal holiday in an apartment is accompanied by practical hotel services. The guest decides, entirely on an individual basis, how often the rooms are cleaned, when he needs fresh towels, whether a child carer is required at short notice, when he wishes to eat in the hotel restaurant, when a delivery service or a sport and leisure service should be booked. Thus, in such a way each person always only pays for that particular luxury that he really wishes to have. The atmosphere within the grounds really does compare with that in a real village: There is a market place, several sports facilities and playgrounds, barbecue and sitting areas, village shop and bicycle hire, and even a children's and youth club. In this way the Dorfhotel also compliments the benefits of the Rantum locality, particularly through many facilities on offer such as the village shop or the spa available to everyone. Village life can be so pleasant and a holiday in the Dorfhotel Sylt can be so relaxing.

DORFHOTEL SYLT
Hafenstraße 1a
25980 Sylt / OT Rantum
Telefon 046 51 / 46 09-0
info@dorfhotel-sylt.com
www.dorfhotel-sylt.com

Eine Auszeit in Rantums Dünen

An Rantums Steilküste, hoch oben in den Dünen, steht – wie ein Relikt aus alten Zeiten – ein großes weißes, reetgedecktes Haus. Es wirkt perfekt an diesem Ort, so als sei es schon immer da gewesen, dabei aber nie gealtert. Es ist der Söl'ringhof von Gastgeber und Zwei-Sterne-Koch Johannes King, vor einigen Jahren neu errichtet auf den Grundmauern eines alten Friesenhauses. Das Fünf-Sterne-Hotel bietet 15 Zimmer beziehungsweise Suiten verschiedener Kategorie und Größe, teilweise als Maisonette. Die Ausstattung ist immer exklusiv und originell: In einigen Zimmern kann der Gast etwa von der Badewanne aus aufs Meer schauen oder fernsehen. Und wer sich dort oder im Wellnessbereich entspannt hat, kann das berühmte hauseigene Sterne-Restaurant der Küchenchefs Philipp Berner und Johannes King besuchen. Luxus ist in solch einem Hotel wichtig, aber King will vor allem, dass der Gast sich wie in einem neuen Zuhause fühlt und dennoch Überraschendes erlebt. Er soll sich geborgen vorkommen und dabei trotzdem von neuen Eindrücken begeistern lassen. Johannes King ist glücklich über sein Team, eine perfekte Mischung aus Allroundern und Spezialisten: „Wenn ein Gast zum Beispiel beim Frühstück sitzt, kann er davon ausgehen, dass wir auch da Leute haben, die ihre Aufgabe regelrecht lieben. Hier arbeitet niemand nur, weil es sein Job ist." Und das hat Einfluss auf die Atmosphäre des Hauses. Jeder Mitarbeiter wohnt einmal im Söl'ringhof, allein um diesen Geist spüren zu können.

TIME OFF IN RANTUM'S DUNES

Along Rantum's steep coastline, high among the dunes, there stands – like a relic from times past – a large, white thatched-roof house. Its effect is perfect at this place, as if it had always been here but had at the same time never aged. It is the hotel Söl'ring Hof of host and two-star chef Johannes King, which was built up on the foundations of an old Frisian building several years ago. This five-star hotel offers 15 rooms and suites in various categories and sizes, some as maisonettes. The fixtures and fittings are always exclusive and original: In some of the rooms the guest can even look out to sea from the bathtub, or watch television from it. And those who are relaxing in the hotel or in its wellness area, can also visit the renowned in-house star-rated restaurant of the chefs de cuisine Philipp Berner and Johannes King. Luxury is important in such a hotel, but King desires above all that their guests feel as if they are in a second home but can nevertheless experience something quite surprising. A guest should feel snug and secure and at the same time still be ready to be inspired by new impressions. Johannes King is pleased with his team, a perfect mixture of all-rounders and specialists: "When a guest is for instance sitting down to breakfast, he can assume that we also have people who downright love their role there. There is no-one here just because it is his job". And this has an impact on the atmosphere at the hotel. Each member of staff resides in Söl'ring Hof at least once, simply to be able to witness this spirit.

DORINT SÖL'RING HOF RANTUM
Geschäftsführer: Johannes King
Am Sandwall 1
25980 Sylt / OT Rantum
Telefon: 046 51/83 62 00
info.soelringhof@dorint.com
www.soelring-hof.de

Lieblingsprodukte für Gourmets

Die Zeit zwischen Frühstück und Abendbrot ist ideal, um im Genuss-Shop in Keitum haltzumachen. An dem weißen Friesenhaus prangt der Namenszug von Johannes King. Der Zwei-Sterne-Koch und seine Frau Selina Müller-King haben diesen kleinen Laden mit Bistro 2013 eröffnet, etwa auf halber Strecke zwischen ihrem Bauernhof in Morsum und Kings Hotel Söl'ringhof in Rantum. Hier gibt's es ihre Lieblingsprodukte, regionale und internationale Gourmetspezialitäten, meist originell verpackt, sowie ausgewählte Küchenutensilien. Gemeinsamer Nenner: eine herausragende Qualität, die Johannes King selbst begeistert. Die kleine Bistro-Speisekarte ist ebenfalls nicht alltäglich. Man kann die stets frischen saisonalen Gerichte mit einem guten Wein ganz zwanglos am Tisch drinnen oder draußen genießen. Manches wird – innerhalb Sylts – sogar nach Hause geliefert. Das meiste aus dem Genuss-Shop lässt sich natürlich sowieso mit nach Hause nehmen, und für den kleinen Trost nach Urlaubsende gibt es dann noch den Onlineshop. Ganz gleich, was es einem angetan hat, die rote Polenta aus dem Tessin, Marcona-Mandeln aus Spanien, der exklusiv gelieferte Kaviar aus Frankreich oder Kings selbst gemachte Marmelade aus der Sylter Rose – das Entscheidende: Man hört so manche Geschichte zu den einladend präsentierten und servierten Dingen und versteht, dass kein Produkt zufällig in den Genuss-Shop kommt, sondern Teil der kulinarischen Philosophie Johannes Kings ist. Und so macht alles doppelt Spaß!

FAVOURITE PRODUCTS FOR GOURMETS

The time between breakfast and supper is ideal to stop off at the Genuss-Shop (shop of delights) in Keitum. The name resplendent on the facade of this white Frisian building is of Johannes King. The two-star chef and his wife Selina Müller-King opened this small business with a bistro in 2013, situated about half way between their farmhouse in Morsum and King's Hotel Söl'ringhof in Rantum. You will find your favourite products here, regional and international gourmet specialities, usually packaged in an original way, as well as selected kitchen utensils. The common thread: outstanding quality, which delights Johannes King himself. The small bistro menu is also not an everyday item. Quite unconstrained, one can enjoy the ever fresh seasonal dishes with a fine wine at a table inside or outside. Some things – within the island's limits – can even be delivered. The majority of items in the Genuss-Shop can of course be taken home, and as a small consolation at the end of the holiday there is still the online shop. No matter what has proved so impressive, red polenta from Ticino, Marcona almonds from Spain, exclusively delivered caviar from France or King's own home made Sylt-rose marmalade – the decisive factor is: One hears many a story about the the invitingly presented things that are served up, and understands that none of the products are in the Genuss-Shop by chance, but are all part of Johannes King's culinary philosophy. So, this makes it all twice as much fun!

GENUSS-SHOP JOHANNES KING
Geschäftsführerin:
Selina Müller-King
Gurtstig 2
25980 Sylt / OT Keitum
Telefon: 046 51/96 77 79-0
mail@johannesking.de
www.johannesking.de/
genuss-shop-keitum

1558

Vive la Sylt

Westerland, 20 Uhr MESZ: Eine ältere Dame beugt sich in einen der Strandkörbe, die hier, aufs Meer ausgerichtet, oben auf der Promenade stehen: „Entschuldigen Sie, das ist mein Strandkorb, den habe ich gemietet, könnten Sie bitte aussteigen?" Zum Beweis zieht die Frau noch ihre Quittung hervor. Folgsam, aber leicht zerknirscht erhebt sich ein Pärchen und geht hinunter an den Strand, auf der Suche nach einem neuen Plätzchen für sich, ihren Pinot Grigio und den Sonnenuntergang. Eine Szene, so alltäglich wie ein Stein im Schuh oder ein vergessener Sonnenhut. Dennoch gibt es immer wieder Diskussionen, wie man den Umgang mit den Körben denn besser regeln könne. Manche wünschen sich gar prinzipiell freie Körbe für alle, schließlich zahle man ja genug Kurtaxe, finden sie. Andere stört es, dass jemand etwas umsonst bekommt, für das sie bezahlen müssen, ganz egal, ob der Korb gerade gebraucht wird oder nicht. Während abschließbare Strandkörbe in anderen Nord- und Ostseebädern der Normalfall sind, bleibt es auf Sylt auch da beim Appell an die Vernunft. Die meisten Sylter und ihre Gäste halten es einfach lieber mit der Philosophie des leben und leben lassen. Das passt ja auch ganz gut zu einem Ort, der wie kaum ein anderer, Menschen mit den unterschiedlichsten Interessen anspricht. Denn je mehr Verständnis da ist, desto weniger Verbote sind nötig, und das ist ebenfalls ein Stück Erholung – genauso wie der Strandkorb selbst, der übrigens auch jederzeit online reserviert werden kann!

VIVE LA SYLT

Westerland, 20:00pm CEST: A somewhat older lady ducks into one of the canopied wicker beach chairs up here on the promenade facing the sea: "Excuse me! That's my beach chair, I hired it, could you please get another?" As a form of proof, she even pulls out her docket. Obedient but a little contrite, the young pair gets up and they stroll down to the beach on the look-out for another nice place for themselves, their Pinot Grigio and the setting sun. A scene as commonplace as a breath of air or as a misplaced sun hat. There are nevertheless discussions every so often as to how the question of the beach chairs could be better organised. In principle, some even desire free beach chairs for everyone. They say that one ultimately pays enough spa tax in any case. Others are annoyed that they have to pay for someone else receiving something for nothing, never mind whether the beach chair is in use or not. While lockable beach chairs are quite common in other North Sea and Baltic bathing locations, on Sylt it rather remains an appeal to common sense. The majority of Sylt natives and their guests simply hold on to the philosophy of live and let live. This fits very well indeed with a place that, unlike almost any other, appeals to people with the most diverse interests, because the more 'reason' there exists, then the less need there is for a 'verbot' and that is in itself a little relaxing – just like the beach chair itself, which can, by the way, be reserved online at any time!

INSEL SYLT TOURISMUS-SERVICE GMBH
Strandstraße 35
25980 Sylt / OT Westerland
Telefon: 046 51 / 99 80
www.insel-sylt.de

Ein schöner Tag auf Sylt geht zu Ende. Bei allem, was man hier machen kann, der Blick aufs Meer bleibt doch das Beste.
A beautiful day on Sylt comes to an end. Of all the things that can be experienced here, a view out to sea is still the best.

Adressverzeichnis
List of addresses

Bäckereien & Konditoreien

BÄCKEREI & KONDITOREI INGWERSEN 82
Jürgen Ingwersen GmbH & Co. KG
Terpstig 76
25980 Sylt / OT Morsum
Telefon 046 51 / 82 33 42
info@ingwersen-sylt.de
www.ingwersen-sylt.de

BÄCKEREI RAFFELHÜSCHEN
GMBH & CO. KG 68
Geschäftsführer: Broder Raffelhüschen,
Thomas Raffelhüschen
Zum Fliegerhorst 20
25980 Sylt / OT Tinnum
Telefon 046 51 / 223 78
www.raffelhueschen-sylt.de

BÄCKEREI & KONDITOREI SPECK 30
Inhaber: Holger Speck
Süderweg 1
25999 Kampen
Telefon 046 51 / 425 60
speck-baeckerei@web.de
www.baeckerei-speck.de

Feinkost & Delikatessen

GENUSS-SHOP JOHANNES KING 124
Geschäftsführerin:
Selina Müller-King
Gurtstig 2
25980 Sylt / OT Keitum
Telefon 046 51 / 967 77 90
mail@johannesking.de
www.johannesking.de/genuss-shop-keitum

SYLTER MEERSALZMANUFAKTUR 24
Sylter Meersalz GmbH & Co. KG
Hafenstraße 2
25992 List
Telefon 046 51 / 942 90 74
kontakt@sylter-meersalz.de
www.sylter-meersalz.de

Galerien

GALERIE HEROLD 34
Braderuper Weg 4
25999 Kampen
Telefon: 046 51 / 451 35
herold@galerie-herold.de
www.galerie-herold.de

Bahnhofstraße 4
25980 Sylt / OT Keitum
Telefon 046 51 / 446 55 50
katharina@galerie-herold.de
www.galerie-herold.de

Garten & Floristik

ALTE WÄSCHEREI 108
Kirchenweg 9
25980 Sylt / OT Westerland
Telefon 046 51 / 835 20 20
www.altewaescherei.com

GRUEN+/SYLT.......... 98
Inhaber: Jens Reichel
Kollundweg 20
25980 Sylt / OT Westerland
Telefon 01 72 / 860 11 18
info@gruenplus-sylt.de
www.gruenplus-sylt.de

Haustiere

PROMENADENMISCHUNG 60
Stefanie Hausen
Hauptstraße 8–10
25996 Wennigstedt
Telefon 046 51 / 967 66 70
info@promenadenmischung-sylt.de
www.promenadenmischung-sylt.de

Hotels

Immobilien & Vermietung

Adressverzeichnis
List of addresses

Inneneinrichtung

HOMESTORIES OHG 94
Ramona Dreessen und Ralf Langmaack
Andreas-Nielsen-Straße 10
25980 Sylt / OT Westerland
Telefon 046 51 / 995 27 76
mail@homestories.cc
www.homestories.cc

Juweliere & Goldschmiede

DÜNNE KAMPEN 44
Westerweg 14
25999 Kampen
Telefon 046 51 / 434 83
duenne-kampen@web.de
www.duenne-kampen.de

JUWELIER H. SPLIEDT SYLT GMBH 32
Torsten H. Spliedt
Hauptstraße 15
25999 Kampen
Telefon 046 51 / 410 01
info@spliedt-sylt.de
www.spliedt-sylt.de

Mode & Accessoires

KEGELMANN 50
Markus Kastenhuber GmbH
Kurhausstraße 2
25999 Kampen
Telefon 046 51 / 429 04
www.kastenhuber-sylt.de

STEFFI-MODEN 104
H. A. Gülcher GmbH
Friedrichstraße 35
25980 Sylt / OT Westerland
Telefon 046 51 / 231 22
info@steffi-moden.de
www.steffi-moden.de

Restaurants, Cafés & Bars

AUSTERNSTUBE SYLTER ROYAL 18
Dittmeyer´s Austern-Compagnie GmbH
Hafenstraße 10–12
25992 List
Telefon 046 51 / 87 75 25
www.sylter-royal.de

RESTAURANT ALTES ZOLLHAUS SYLT GMBH 100
Geschäftsführer: Oliver Suchy
Boysenstraße 18
25980 Sylt / OT Westerland
Telefon 046 51 / 44 94 43
info@altes-zollhaus-sylt.de
www.altes-zollhaus-sylt.de

BEACH BOX SYLT – BURGER BUDE 96
Lars Oliver Witte
Käpt'n-Christiansen-Straße 42
25908 Sylt / OT Westerland

RESTAURANT COAST 118
Familie Rose
Stiindeelke 2
25980 Sylt / OT Rantum
Telefon 046 51 / 15 51
info@restaurant-coast.de
www.restaurant-coast.de

IVO & CO. BISTRO UND WEINE 62
Inhaber: Nico Torbahn
Seestrasse 29
25996 Wenningstedt
Telefon 0 46 51 / 99 56 76 9
info@ivoundco-bistro.de
www.ivoundco-bistro.de

BROT & BIER 74
Gastronomischer Gastgeber: Alexandro Pape
Gurtstig 1
25980 Sylt / OT Keitum
Telefon 046 51 / 936 37 43
reservierung@brot-und-bier.de
www.brot-und-bier.de

EISCAFÉ VENEZIA 22
Mario Hodak
Am Hafen 20
25992 List
Telefon 046 51 / 449 52 18

KLEINE KÜCHENKATE 80
Familie Sprengkamp
Hoyerstig 2
25980 Sylt / OT Keitum
Telefon 046 51 / 333 87
info@kleinekuechenkate.de
www.kleinekuechenkate.de

KLEINER BRUDER – BAR LOUNGE 110
Enrico Schulze
Böttcherstraße 3
25980 Sylt / OT Westerland
Telefon 046 51 / 804 98 74
willkommen@kleinerbruder.net
www.kleinerbruder.net

Reisen & Verkehr

INSEL SYLT TOURISMUS-SERVICE GMBH 126
Strandstraße 35
25980 Sylt / OT Westerland
Telefon 046 51 / 99 80
www.insel-sylt.de

Sport & Freizeit

KITESCHULE SYLT 16
Philipp Brückmann
Am Ellenbogen
25992 List
Telefon 01 72 / 472 17 48
info@kiteschule-sylt.de
www.kiteschule-sylt.de

YOUKSAKKA BOW & FUNCOMPANY 70
Keitumer Landstraße am Sportzentrum Sylt-Ost
25980 Sylt / OT Tinnum
Telefon 01 77 / 802 73 09
info@youksakka.de
www.youksakka.de

Wellness & Beauty

AKZENTE – PARFÜMERIE & BEAUTY 106
Friedrichstraße 29-31
25980 Sylt / OT Westerland
Telefon 046 51 / 835 02 50
service@akzenteplus.de
www.akzenteplus.de

BESONDERE ADRESSEN FÜR SIE ENTDECKT

LUXEMBURG

224 Seiten, Hardcover, dt./frz.
978-3-86528-896-7

HAMBURG UND DAS ALTE LAND

152 Seiten, Hardcover
978-3-86528-887-5

EIFEL & OSTBELGIEN

160 Seiten, Hardcover
978-3-86528-879-0

FASZINATION WELTERBE – DEUTSCHLANDS SÜDEN

176 Seiten, Hardcover
978-3-86528-854-7

SCHÄTZE AUS DER PFALZ

208 Seiten, Hardcover
978-3-86528-493-8

SCHÄTZE BODENSEE UND OBERSCHWABEN

192 Seiten, Hardcover
978-3-86528-556-9

TRENDS & LIFESTYLE BREMEN

128 Seiten, Hardcover
978-3-86528-891-2

TRENDS & LIFESTYLE INNSBRUCK

128 Seiten, Hardcover
978-3-86528-895-0

LEBEN, WOHNEN & GENIESSEN OLDENBURG

128 Seiten, Hardcover
978-3-86528-897-4

GÄRTEN IM TESSIN

156 Seiten, Hardcover
978-3-86528-867-7

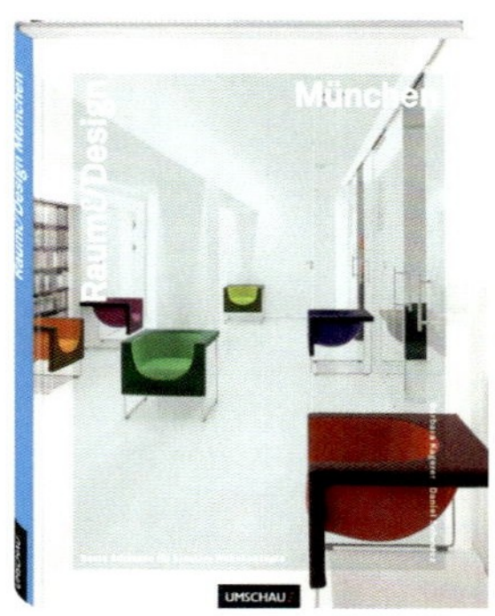

RAUM & DESIGN MÜNCHEN

184 Seiten, Hardcover
978-3-86528-546-1

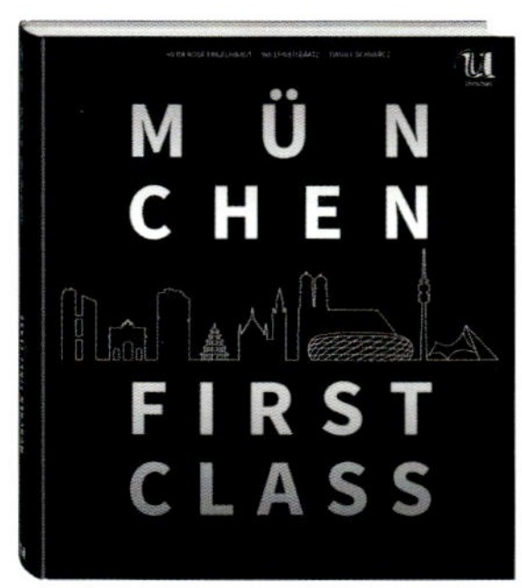

MÜNCHEN FIRST CLASS

152 Seiten, Hardcover, dt./engl.
978-3-86528-888-2

WEITERE EMPFEHLUNGEN FÜR SIE

WIR HABEN EINFACH GEKOCHT
100 Erinnerungen an Lieblingsrezepte
304 Seiten, Hardcover
978-3-86528-805-9

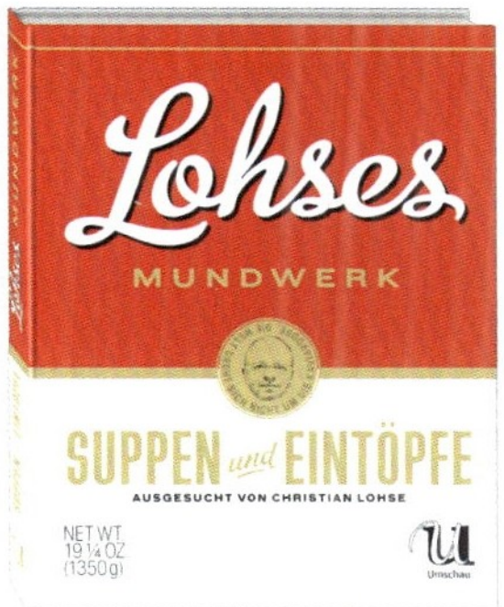

LOHSES MUNDWERK
Suppen und Eintöpfe ausgesucht
von Christian Lohse
248 Seiten, Hardcover
978-3-86528-695-6

WILD
130 Rezepte für jeden Tag
256 Seiten, Hardcover
mit Lesebändchen
978-3-86528-734-2

GRILLEN – TASTE OF ASIA
144 Seiten, Softcover
978-3-86528-810-3

DRUNTER & DRÜBER
Das Brotbackbuch &
Das Aufstrichbuch
208 Seiten, Hardcover
978-3-86528-746-5

MARTHA'S SALAD
Fünfzig Salate to go
144 Seiten, Hardcover mit
Banderole und 12 Aufklebern
978-3-86528-808-0

Neuer Umschau Buchverlag GmbH
Moltkestraße 14
D-67433 Neustadt/Weinstraße
Telefon + 49 (0) 63 21 / 877-833
Telefax + 49 (0) 63 21 / 877-859

info@umschau-buchverlag.de
Neuer Umschau Buchverlag
Umschau_Verlag
umschauverlag

www.umschau-verlag.de

Impressum
Imprint

Neustadt an der Weinstraße
1. Auflage 2016

RECHERCHE **RESEARCH**
Sabine Vatterodt, Hamburg

TEXTE **TEXTS**
Frank Wagner, Hamburg
frankwagner.hamburg@gmx.de
Frank Wagner stammt von der Nordseeküste, aus Cuxhaven; Studium der Germanistik und Publizistik in Göttingen und München; heute ist er freier Autor und Journalist in Hamburg. Er liebt die kreative Arbeit mit Menschen, Worten und Geschichten.
Frank Wagner comes from the North Sea coast, from Cuxhaven. He graduated in German philology and publishing studies in Göttingen and Munich. He is now an independent author and journalist in Hamburg. He loves creative collaborations with other people, with words and with stories.

Wir bedanken uns für die freundlicherweise zur Verfügung gestellten Texte bei:
We wish to express our thanks to the following for kindly making their texts available to us:
Teekontor Keitum (Seiten **pages** 77, 78)

FOTOS **PHOTOGRAPHY**
Markus Tollhopf, Hamburg
www.tollhopf.de
Markus Tollhopf, aufgewachsen im Hessischen, Grafik-Design-Studium in Kassel, lebt und arbeitet in und von Hamburg aus. Neben Buchproduktionen fotografiert er Architektur und Stills, ist gerne unterwegs, um Neues zu entdecken und ablichten zu dürfen.
Markus Tollhopf grew up in Hessen, in Kassel, and later also studied graphic design there. He lives and works in and from Hamburg. Along with book productions, he photographs architecture and produces stills, he is happy to be on the move in order to discover anew, and to simply enjoy photography.

Wir bedanken uns für die freundlicherweise zur Verfügung gestellten Fotos bei:
We wish to express our thanks to the following for kindly providing photographs:
Mathis Höft / Dünne Kampen (Seiten **pages** 44, 45)

LEKTORAT, GESTALTUNG UND PRODUKTION **EDITING, DESIGN AND PRODUCTION**
Marc Strittmatter
ppp.services, München
info@ppp.services

UMSCHLAGGESTALTUNG **COVERDESIGN**
Atelier Seidel Verlagsgrafik, Teising
www.atelier-seidel.de

KORREKTORAT **PROOFREADING**
Renate Nöldeke, München

ÜBERSETZUNGEN **TRANSLATIONS**
Jonathan Smale, Heidelberg

KARTE **MAP**
Thorsten Trantow, Herbolzheim
www.trantow-atelier.de

LITHOGRAFIE **REPRODUCTION**
Blaschke Vision, Laubach / Wetterfeld

DRUCK UND VERARBEITUNG **PRINTING, BINDING AND FINISHING**
NINO Druck GmbH, Neustadt an der Weinstraße
www.ninodruck.de

Printed in Germany
ISBN 978-3-86528-921-6

Besuchen Sie uns im Internet:
Visit us at our web site:
www.umschau-verlag.de

Angela Pajec

Außer Kontrolle

Ein Münster Krimi

agenda